verses *we know* by *heart*

discovering the details of familiar Old Testament passages

By
Jennifer Devlin

I0805546

randall house
114 Bush Rd | Nashville, TN 37217
randallhouse.com

Verses We Know By Heart

Published by Randall House Publications
114 Bush Road
Nashville, TN 37217

Printed in the United States of America

10-ISBN 0892655658

13-ISBN 9780892655656

To the love of my life, Bob, who encourages me every moment

as I seek to remain in the middle of God's will.

Thank you for walking this journey with me.

Welcome Friend!

I'm so honored to have you join me on this six-week adventure through some of our most favorite Old Testament passages. You'll find that the focus verses we will study together are quite familiar...they might even be *verses you know by heart!* In fact, my hope is that the *verses you know by heart* will become a springboard to understanding whole passages of Scripture. My desire is to see you continuing to pursue reading and studying God's Word in greater measure with each passing day. But before we begin our study, I want to share my heart about the motivation behind this Bible study concept.

If we took a field trip to our local mall and surveyed the shoppers, asking what their favorite Old Testament verses were, we would find many of the people quoting a relatively short list of verses. As a society of faith that relies on a brief list of familiar phrases, we tend to build a shallow arsenal of defenses against the enemy. Quoting the same verses over and over, whether they truly apply to the situation or not, results in a sound-byte religious experience. The sound-byte approach gives us just enough of the Bible to sound good, but not quite enough to live on.

How did this mini quote approach evolve? I propose it is due to our culture's drive to perfect the art of "busy." Busy lives require quick solutions. Quick solutions bring forth creative answers. Creative answers come in all shapes and sizes. Supply is meeting demand, even in today's Christian retail outlets.

While all these retail items and quick Scripture reminders are a wonderful addition to our walk with the Lord, a question we must ask ourselves is this: *do we read more Scripture in sound-bytes than passages straight from the Word?* Are we wearing a t-shirt and sticking a bumper sticker on our car *instead* of reading God's Word? If so, then we are subscribing to a sound-byte approach to the Bible. I pray that we all would desire a deeper relationship with Jesus Christ, and develop an insatiable passion for His Word that goes way beyond our quick Scripture fixes.

In this six-week journey together, we will dive into Bible passages that include some of our favorite Old Testament verses. We'll catch a glimpse of the deeper meaning and context of these tidbits from the Bible, better understanding of what God meant to say, how that passage was originally used, and ways that we can practically apply those truths to our lives. Did I miss some of your favorite Old Testament verses? I challenge you to look them up, read the entire passage, and go through the same process we have used for these six weeks. Continue your journey of discovery!

I simply can do nothing without the grace, mercy, love, and power of my Savior Jesus Christ. Thank You for sending the Holy Spirit to equip me as I follow You. Thank You for letting me share Your truth with the nations.

A big thanks goes out to Bonnie and Owen – many days of patience and help have not gone unnoticed. I love you guys!

Emily, Michelle, and Gwen – thanks for helping me get this manuscript ready. God has blessed me with such sweet friends to work with.

Reader, let me take a minute right here to praise God for *you*. I thank Him for your desire to know Jesus in a greater way, and I pray that the words in this book will lead you to His feet. Dive head first into an extravagant love affair with Jesus, and never settle for just a little bit of Scripture.

Pursuing God with you,

Jennifer

WEEK ONE

Creator God

In the Beginning...

Genesis 1:1-2:3

God created. Long before any culture or religious camp began discussing the timing of events in the creation story, one fact stood firm: the God of the Universe decided to speak the world, stars, sun, moon, and everything we know into being. God created. Centuries after this absolute fact, humans have taken up debate (and at times even heated argument) in a feeble attempt to articulate what the almighty God has already spoken; He was there in the beginning and He formed the world, all that is in it, and all that we see in the heavens.

Without our input, intellect, or personal requests, the Lord spoke forth our existence, and filled our environment with beautiful creatures and necessary resources. He designed our world with scenery and landscapes that would intrigue our souls and cause us to venture out in search of the unusual beauty of far-off lands. The most exotic flora and fauna all began in the creative mind of the Father. We, as God's human race, have a deeply ingrained passion to view and experience the vast intricacies of the creation that was formed and filled for God's pleasure.

Each New Year's Eve, individuals make countless personal resolutions involving the promise to read the entire Bible in a year. These individuals study reading plans, they purchase special Bibles, and their best laid plans begin. What is the first line most of these reading schedules feature? You guessed it. Genesis 1:1.

Many ambitious readers step into their resolution journey with the memorable words of our focus verse, "In the beginning . . ." passing before their eyes and resonating into their minds. But does that truth *register* in the heart of the reader? Unfortunately, it is far too easy to glide over a familiar passage without stopping to take in a deeper understanding of a well-known theme. In light of this, in our first lesson we will learn a bit more about God's account of creation than the usual drive-by glimpse can give.

I imagine that many of you, at this moment, may be itching to write down the sequence of days and the categories of new creatures and environmental additions. You know them all by heart. This series of events is crucial to our faith. (If it weren't, God wouldn't have included it in His Word.) We will spend this chapter going over the familiar list. As we travel through the first week of our world's story, we will also look into the "God story" within the lines of Scripture. There is an underlying truth that far surpasses the usual creation sequence checklist. It is the powerful truth that God wanted us. He created mankind, the creatures, and our surroundings because He loves us. As we study this critical topic, I propose we accept the following challenge: *Let's take God at His Word.* Let's believe God and what His love letter tells us.

DAY ONE

THE STORY UNFOLDS – GENESIS 1:1-8

The Focus Verse:

In the beginning God created the heavens and the earth. **Genesis 1:1**

The Main Thought:

God created.

The Story within the Story:

I don't remember my first moments of life after birth, or my beginning days in the world, but my parents spent years remembering the moment-by-moment account. They gladly recounted the joy of childbirth and the fruits of my mother's labor all wrapped up in a pink and blue blanket provided by the hospital. My mother distinctly remembered the sound of my first cry, my eyes as they were beginning to open, and my mouth as it widened in anticipation of food. She loved to describe the way my little pink fingers and toes looked as she counted each one. Delighted with the child the Lord had given them, and filled with joy at the creation they held in their hands, my parents etched that event into their collection of memories.

When my husband and I found out we were going to have a child, we were ecstatic. The nine months of pregnancy seemed to be without end, and then his birth day came. With a quick pop my water broke and we were rushing to the hospital. We weren't the only ones in a hurry; apparently our new child was eager to join us and didn't want to wait a minute longer. With the nurse shouting to my husband to help wheel my hospital bed into the delivery room, I was speeding into the next stage of my life before I knew what hit me. And then, we welcomed him to the world; his cry, ten fingers and ten toes—the miracle of our newborn son. What a wonderful morning that was, even in the midst of the panic and pain.

Although our son Owen obviously doesn't remember the day he was born, he likes to tell others about it because he was born in a foreign country. With dual citizenship and two birth certificates, he is a child who has an interesting story to tell. While his first certificate came from his birth country, the official certificate came from the country of his primary citizenship. We remember the moments, the story, and the details, but in the end, he knows he's an American. We love to tell the story, as most families do. Imagine how much God loves to tell the story of the days He created the world!

God remembers the days He spent forming the world, carefully and intentionally putting each creature in the new environment, and purposefully speaking every living thing into being. Just as our parents describe our first moments to anyone who asks, our Father in heaven has preserved our world's birth story for all generations in His Word. The scrapbook of humanity's journey holds the earth's story in high esteem, sharing the details of creation before any other truth. Our parents were present at the beginning of our lives, and God was present at the birth of creation. The gift of the earth's story is available to all nations through the first pages of Scripture.

The Passage:

Read Genesis 1:1-8. Write down key points from the text and journal your thoughts about what you have read:

The Details:

1. In Genesis 1:1, what did God create?

2. Genesis 1:2 describes a few things. First, what was the earth like before God created?

The second part of verse 2 reveals a clue about the Holy Spirit's role in the creation story. What was He doing in this verse?

Here in verse 2, the Holy Spirit has been actively involved in God's story from the first moments of life until now. We will discover more about this relationship with God and the Holy Spirit at the end of today's segment.

3. What was the first thing God said, as shown in verse 3? What did the Lord do as a result of His first words?

4. In verse 5, what was light called? What was darkness called?

Did you notice that the sun and the moon have not been created yet, but the day and night cycle has been established? Why do you think light and dark, day and night, are created before the sun and the moon, and what significance do you think this has?

Before the sun and moon were placed in the sky above, God spoke forth light in the darkness. He separated the light out of the darkness. The original Hebrew word for light, *'or*, refers to illumination or lighting. *The Complete Word Study Dictionary: Old Testament* edited by Warren Baker and Eugene Carpenter explains 'or as "light itself" in this passage, and "is used primarily to refer to light from heavenly bodies." (p. 27) Within this definition, Baker and Carpenter mention that "light is always used as a positive symbol, such as for good fortune." God is the giver of light, and the source of our joy and victory. He dispels the darkness, and draws us to His glorious presence through our relationship with Him.

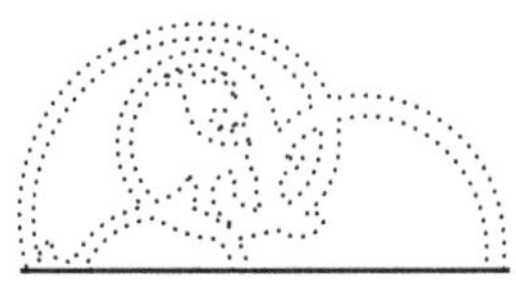

When God separated the waters, He created a shelf of water in the atmosphere, and left a large amount of water on the earth's surface. That shelf or firmament of water, above the earth, was released during the Flood in Noah's day.

5. Genesis 1:6-8 details the second day of the creation account. What was spoken into existence on the second day?

What did God separate in verse 7? What was the expanse in the middle called (verse 8)?

The atmosphere was created, and God was beginning the process of establishing the perfect environment for sustaining life. Waters, sky, shelter from the elements of the universe, and the system for climate control and oxygen were setting the stage. The earth was ready for the next step in God's creation timeline. Tomorrow we will learn about land and seed bearing plants.

A Closer Look:

The Godhead is lovingly revealed in the first chapter of Genesis, with the three parts of the Trinity shown through:

- God the Father creating,
- The Holy Spirit hovering over the waters,
- Jesus, as the Word of God, being spoken forth.

What confirmation do we have that Jesus was present during the Creation of the world? John the Apostle records in John 1:1-3 the following:

> In the beginning was the Word, and the Word was with God, and the Word was God. He was in the beginning with God. All things came into being through Him, and apart from Him nothing came into being that has come into being.

Jesus was not only there, He was integral to the creation process. Nothing happened without Jesus. Together, the three equal parts of the Godhead were actively working together in perfect unity forming and creating, speaking and hovering.

A Question for Your Life Today:

In light of our evolution-centered culture, how does this chapter's study of God's creation impact your view on the theory of evolution?

____

____

____

DAY TWO

THE LAND BRINGS FORTH SEED – GENESIS 1:9-13

The Focus Verse:

The earth brought forth vegetation, plants yielding seed after their kind. Genesis 1:12

The Main Thought:

God begins the planting season.

The Story within the Story:

Have you ever lived near a farming community? Our family has had the opportunity to live in a few different rural areas, some focusing on dairy farming, others on planting corn and various cash crops, and now, we find ourselves sitting in high cotton. We currently reside in a wonderful area filled with a blend of new residents and long-time farming dynasties. What used to be completely dedicated to farmland has transformed into a commuter's paradise—a landscape filled with peaceful living, lower building prices, and beautiful sunsets. Our county's houses have grown in the place of the cotton in many of the fields, and many times at a quicker pace than an average cotton season.

The variety we see in our local population is confirmed through the range of interests, jobs, and uses of the land around us. From ball fields to shopping centers, cotton gins to cropland, our area boasts a diversity I've not previously experienced. Yet somehow, the landscape flows with a peaceful unity that pleases the eye.

During my daily commute, I find myself continually fascinated by the crops on the side of the road. In the midst of traffic, subdivisions, strip malls, and suburban life, cotton is tucked into the remaining land in planned fields; planted in tight, deliberate rows. The selection of vehicles rambling down the main roads are becoming as integrated as the roadside views. One day you might be driving behind the newest sports car, the following day you may be slowed down a bit by construction vehicles, and the next you may find yourself stuck behind a huge green field monster (a combine, tractor, or other farming machine) that chugs from one field to the next on the only road available—the commuter's thoroughfare.

From the early days of spring to the Indian summer moments of autumn, the farming fields go through massive transformation. Workers tend the fields, harvest the crops, and prepare for the next year's crop, never giving the construction, congestion, and store customers a second thought. The goal is to raise cotton. The method is the same as it has always been. Plant the seeds, watch them grow, harvest and prepare for next year. While the machinery and techniques for harvesting have developed over the centuries, the basic system and season of growth established by God's design of plant life began on the third day of creation.

The Passage:

Read Genesis 1:9-13. Write down key points from the text and journal your thoughts about what you have read:

The Details:

1. According to Genesis 1:9, how did the dry land appear?

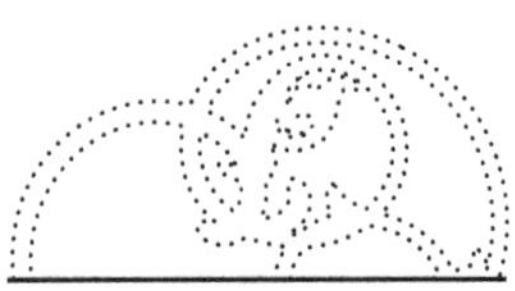

In order to reveal the land, the Lord "gathered" the waters into one area, revealing the land beneath.

2. In verse 10, we see how God labeled the water and the land:

Dry land was called ____________________

Water was called ____________________

3. After the water was separated, revealing dry land, what did God create? (Genesis 1:11-12). What interesting details does the Word give us about this portion of God's creation?

In verse 11, the plants and fruit were sprouting, yielding seed and bearing fruit with seed in them. God began the process, and established the ongoing provision through seed with each kind of vegetation.

Take a moment to pray, thanking the Lord for His provision of land and sea, plants and fruit. Look at your lifestyle and imagine how different life would be without the blessing of fruit-filled vegetation, and the provision of seed for growing the plants we need for survival.

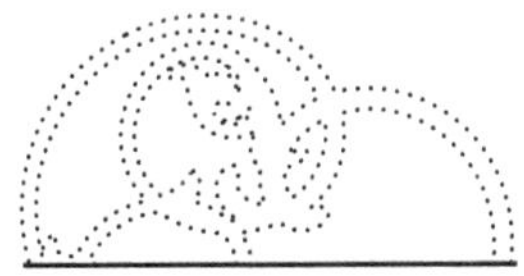

"...plants yielding seed after their kind, and trees bearing fruit with seed in them, after their kind."

Genesis 1:12

A Closer Look:

Before the sun and moon were created, the dry land was revealed and the seed bearing plants were sprouting. All of this was orchestrated at the hand of Almighty God. The plans of the Lord were being accomplished by His power and in His timing.

Notice that the Father not only gave plants, but seeds, to continue growth in a new crop or plant cycle. Fruit also appeared with the vegetation, and the seeds contained in the fruit would also facilitate future growth. Each plant was created "according to their kind." God knew what types of vegetation He desired to create for the earth. Specific kinds of life were created in an orderly way and with purpose, and have kept their distinct qualities for generations. He provided a method to continue their growth through seeds. Our Creator's plan included more than one season of life. God intended to provide a cycle of growth that would continue to sustain for generations.

A Question for Your Life Today:

Since God created the world and all the creatures in the world, and evolutionists believe that the world's creatures simply evolved over time, what would you tell an evolutionist about God, using this week's passage as your reference?

DAY THREE

THE TWINKLING SKY – GENESIS 1:14-19

The Focus Verse:

Then God said, "Let there be lights in the expanse of the heavens to separate the day from the night, and let them be for signs and for seasons and for days and years." **Genesis 1:14**

The Main Thought:

God creates seasons and markers of time.

The Story within the Story:

I attended a high school that had its very own planetarium. As a kid who would rather do anything than chemistry, I was excited to see the option for stargazing hiding in the course descriptions for senior year. *Could it be? Can I get out of high school with credit for taking astronomy instead of chemistry? It's worth a try,* I thought to myself. With the guidance counselor's approval and class schedule in hand, I wove my way through the hallways until I found the subtle enclave with the right room number affixed above the door.

The first day of class, we all filed into the covert hideaway nestled between the library and the main hall. Each row of reclining seats beckoned the new students with a comfort we had not been given in any other class on campus. It was almost too much to bear when the instructor asked us to lean back in reclining chairs in a pitch dark room and look at the projected scene on the ceiling. We all looked at each other and just knew this was the best-kept secret of the school.

For a whole semester, we began our day in easy chairs and dim light—almost as if we were still at home under the covers hitting the snooze button one more time. Amidst the comfort and constant presentations, we learned many things about the universe the Father created, and now I'm grateful for that class. Not only because I could check

a block for graduation, my semester in astronomy gave me memories and a love for the sky that would have eluded me without the need for a high school science credit.

For as long as there have been stars in the sky, there have been people fascinated with the starry hosts in view each night. Centuries of star gazers and galactic researchers have brought us detailed explanations of the placement, qualities, and intricacies of the solar system. While the nighttime display is beautiful and majestic, the excitement for the unknown treasures above the earth's atmosphere has caused quite a stir. In their zeal for understanding the things above, some people over the ages have misplaced their focus of worship from Creator to the created stellar objects. May we never fall prey to such deception.

We are never to worship the celestial creations. We *are* created to worship the one true God who created the vision we see in the sky. The vastness of the nighttime display pales in comparison to the unending power and majesty of our God. He is big—real big. The Father's presence is greater than the farthest reaches of the universe. As we look to the sky in wonder of sun, moon, and stars above, let us be mindful of the God who gave us the massive display. We have been given each portion of creation for very specific reasons, as we will see with today's lesson.

The Passage:

Read Genesis 1:14-19. Write down key points from the text and journal your thoughts about what you have read:

____

____

____

The Details:

1. Genesis 1:14 tells us so much about the purpose of the lights in the sky. What does Scripture reveal about God's purpose for the sky's display?

____

____

____

2. Verse 15 includes another purpose for the lights. Describe that purpose:

____

____

____

God's display of lights in the heavens give us help with seasons and marking time as well as giving light to the earth. The Hebrew term for light used in verse 14 is the word *ma'or*, a term describing something luminous, and *The Complete Word Study Dictionary: Old Testament* states that this word is also "employed in connection with the lamp in the Tabernacle" and that it is used "to describe the heavenly lights in the creation story of Genesis." (p. 560) God already provided His light, and now, He created heavenly lights to illuminate our lives. Functional, and necessary, but so very different from the light He provided on that very first day. While Jesus is the light of the world, the sun is just a "lump" of light. Quite a difference, isn't it?

3. What do verses 16-19 describe? What things did God create, how did He position them, and why?

____

____

____

We see the Lord designing two types of lights, the sun and the moon, and the stars. He places them in the sky in the perfect position and establishes their seasonal patterns for our use and benefit. God is truly a God of the details! He is concerned with our needs, day or night, summer or winter. As we mark our days and enjoy the changing seasons, may we forever be mindful of the Lord of Hosts who placed each star in the sky and causes the sun to shine into our lives.

A Closer Look:

Isaiah beautifully describes the Lord's part in the creation process like this:

> Lift up your eyes on high and see who has created these *stars*, the One who leads forth their host by number, He calls them all by name; because of the greatness of His might and the strength of His power, not one *of them* is missing (Isaiah 40:26). [*Emphasis added.*]

As we have been studying this week, the Lord is the originator, creator, and master designer of the world around us. With His unending wisdom He has formed and sustained the seasons, environments, and interdependent relationships within our global structure to sustain life on earth. Through today's lesson, we see that the sun, moon, and stars were created after light and darkness. The stellar displays God has provided assist us with marking seasons, time, and daily cycles. He is our source for seasons, time, and weather. Just as we should not look to false myths like astrology predictions and star worship, we cannot let ourselves be talked into using terms like "Mother Nature" and "Father Time." Trusting in such thoughts is as empty as the newspaper's horoscope!

Who can fathom the greatness of God? The stars in the sky are too numerous to count, and the Almighty is without limit and power. Take time tonight to go outside and gaze at the wonder of God's heavenly display. Give Him praise for His provision of seasons, lights and markers for time. As we praise the Lord for marking time, let us always remember Psalm 31:14-15: "But as for me, I trust in You, O LORD, I say, 'You are my God.' My times are in Your hand." No matter what we may face in the many seasons of our lives, the Lord is our strength, and we can be confident that He is trustworthy.

A Question for Your Life Today:

As we have studied the Lord's process of creation, what has impacted you the most? How can that knowledge be incorporated into your daily life, and the way you impact others?

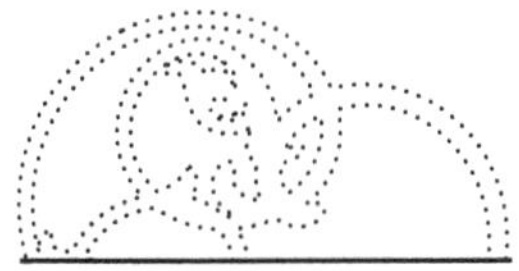

Father God is the master planner of our world's atmosphere, landscape and environment. He designed our plant life and the conditions needed for survival. "Mother Nature" and "Father Time" are nothing more than fabled characters from the mouths of those who do not see the hand of God in the creation story. Again, let us take God at His Word!

DAY FOUR

LIVING CREATURES AND MAN – GENESIS 1:20-31

The Focus Verse:

God created man in His own image, in the image of God He created him; male and female He created them. **Genesis 1:27**

The Main Thought:

God created man and gave him dominion over creation.

The Story within the Story:

Every family has hobbies and activities they enjoy, and ours is particularly fond of visiting zoos and aquariums. No matter where we travel or what state we have lived in, any kind of tourist spot focusing on animals is one of the first things we find. We've seen some pretty exotic examples of the creativity of God, and continue to seek out more examples of the diversity of wildlife. What we pursue in our communities and travel destinations has had an impact on our home as well. We enjoy animals and have talked ourselves into caring for a few within the walls of our home.

Some say that our house is like a mini zoo. With guinea pigs, cockatiels, and two puppies, our lives are full of the joy that comes from enjoying household pets. In the morning we rise and greet our family—both human and animal. *Rise and shine, Son, it's time to get up! Hello birds. Good morning, piggies. Come on puppies, outside we go.* Our routine is predictable and our inclusion of everyone in the morning greeting is common. Before the coffee pot is full of the sunrise brew, we have cheerfully acknowledged *all* the family members; even those who tweet, bark, and squeak.

The golden retriever excitedly retrieves the newspaper from the driveway each morning and the birds continually create new songs and noises to entertain the humans when they enter the room. The piggies love to be cuddled now and again and hop around in the cage when they are happy, adding to the activity in the house. Each of our pets has its own relationship with us, and shows their presence in unique ways. Together, they are a loved part of the family.

God has blessed us with the opportunity to care for a variety of animals. With that blessing comes a family structure. While the dogs may think they rule the house and keeps us in line, the truth of the matter is, the humans are in charge. Dad provides for their needs and has final say. Mom buys the dog food and makes sure it is in the bowl every morning. The boy they love to play with has the responsibility of helping out with the dogs. The family structure is clear and the lines of authority are evident to all. Such a pattern of authority is not a conjured-up plan that man has thought up simply to be in control; it is the result of the foundation God laid in the first six days of creation.

The Passage:

Read Genesis 1:20-31. Write down key points from the text and journal your thoughts about what you have read:

____

____

____

The Details:

1. In Genesis 1:20-22 what were the things God created? What did He command them to do in verse 22?

____

____

____

Not only did the Lord create the birds and sea life, He charged them to fill the earth; providing for the needs of the next portion of the creation story—man.

2. Verse 24 and 25 describe more types of animals that the Father creatively designed for our use and pleasure. What animals are listed in these two verses, and why do you think they were created last?

____

____

____

3. Genesis 1:26 is full of truth for all generations. Look closely at the wording of this verse. Fill in the following blanks:

"Let _______ make man in _______ image, according to _______ likeness …"

The "us" of this verse are the Father, Son and Holy Spirit—another glimpse at the Trinity at work.

"…and let them _______ over the fish of the sea and over the birds of the sky and over the cattle and over _______ the earth, and over every creeping thing that _______ on the earth."

4. Write out Genesis 1:27:

____

____

____

____

In whose image was man created? ________________________

Does that mean we have the same nose, ears, and hair color as God, or does it refer to something else?

____

____

____

Being created in God's image refers to the spirit within us. We are created as spirit beings, capable of choosing relationship with our God. This similarity to God is unique to the human race; no other part of creation carries this distinction. While we resemble Him in some areas such as our spirit nature, we will never equal God completely. He is God, and we are not.

5. What was God's instruction to the humans He created? (1:28)

Man was told to "be ________________ and ________________, and ________________ the earth, and ________________ it; and ________________ over the fish of the sea and over the birds of the sky and over ________________ living thing that moves on the earth."

As God's people, we were created and given authority to be fruitful, multiply, fill, subdue, and rule over the creatures of the earth.

6. In Genesis 1:29-31 God reveals His purpose for creating the creatures and environment around us. What do these verses tell us about God's provision for mankind?

____

____

____

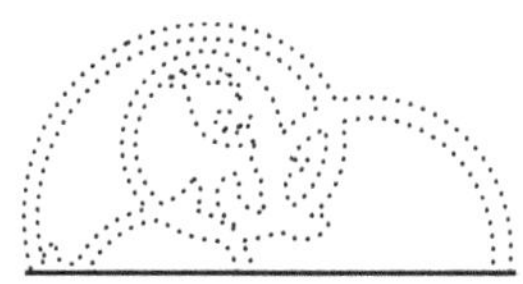

"God saw all that He had made, and behold, it was very good."

Genesis 1:31

God has provided an abundance of resources and supplies to meet our needs for survival and lifestyle as a creation charged to multiply, fill, subdue and rule. The Creator has also provided nourishment for every living creature. He has equipped us to live and provide for those under our care.

A Closer Look:

Since the beginning of time, God has given man authority over the creatures of the earth. This is critical to understand because many of the false religions of the world center on worshiping that which is created instead of the Creator. If we see this truth in Genesis as applicable to our lives today, we will understand more clearly that we are not to worship any animal, person, or created being. God in Heaven is the focus of our worship!

Isaiah 43:21 reminds us that, "The people whom I formed for Myself will declare My praise." We have been created to worship God. We are designed to declare praises to our King! As we gaze on the incredibly diverse animal kingdom through daily life, nature shows, and trips to the zoo, we must be mindful to respect God's structure. No matter how special, costly, or rare the creature, animals must remain subject to the human race. No living thing should ever become more valuable than human life; and no animal should ever be placed in a position to be worshiped.

Even God's people have the danger of falling prey to such misplaced devotion. Exodus 32 records a tragic account involving a worshiper of God Most High and the people who, in his absence, had settled for worshiping idols. While the leader was meeting with the Lord, the people went astray. The followers grew restless and because of their impatience, they compromised true beliefs for the quick fix of a false god.

As Moses descended from his mountaintop meeting with the Lord, holding the Law of the Testimony in his hands, he looked out upon a heartbreaking scene. The people God had called him to lead were worshiping a gold idol made from their own jewelry and fashioned by none other than his priest, Aaron! Moses fumed with anger at the sight of such blatant disrespect for the Lord.

This deception of animal worship isn't limited only to the days of Moses. Paul made a point to explain the cause of animal worship to the New Testament church in Romans 1:21-25:

> "For even though they knew God, they did not honor Him as God or give thanks, but they became futile in their speculations, and their foolish heart was darkened. Professing to be wise, they became fools, and exchanged the glory of the incorruptible God for an image in the form of corruptible man and of birds and four-footed animals and crawling creatures. Therefore God gave them over in the lusts of their hearts to impurity, that their bodies would be dishonored among them. For they exchanged the truth of God for a lie, and worshiped and served the creature rather than the Creator, who is blessed forever. Amen."

Sadly, the same danger of misplaced worship is alive and well today. We, as a body of believers, should feel a deep sadness for the peoples of the world who settle for worshiping something that should be under their authority. In a role reversal, they abdicated their God-given position and gave animals dominion over their lives. As a result of this sadness, we need to intentionally share the gospel with these people groups in order to show them the truth of the one true God of the Bible.

A Question for Your Life Today:

How does it feel to learn that you have dominion over the animals and all creation? As a result of your new understanding, what are some practical ways you can be a better steward of the natural resources and a better caretaker of animals in your life?

____

____

____

____

DAY FIVE

REST – GENESIS 2:1-3

The Focus Verse:

Then God blessed the seventh day and sanctified it, because in it He rested from all His work which God had created and made. **Genesis 2:3**

The Main Thought:

God understands the importance of rest and reflection.

The Story within the Story:

My husband and I have a definite routine on Sunday mornings. No other morning looks quite like Sunday around our house. There is no rush. The television stays off. The worries of the week drift away. The coffee steam swirls above our cups as we sit on our sun porch and read. As the sun rises in the sky, our worries lift off of our minds, giving us a more peaceful outlook on the day.

After lounging and enjoying the sunrise, we get ready and head off to church, visiting with our church family and praising the Lord for who He is and what He means to us. The tranquility of this weekly date is a blessing I don't take lightly. By Friday I am usually longing for that Sunday morning peace. As much as I love this tradition, I realize we aren't the only ones with this kind of routine.

Each Sunday morning, families around the world gather with other believers in the house of the Lord to sing, pray, learn, listen, and have sweet fellowship together. After worship, many of those families congregate around the dinner table to enjoy a meal together. Some, surely more than we realize, follow that meal with a cozy nap on the couch. No other day of the week provides such an opportunity for guilt-free relaxation.

The Sabbath, established by God, is just the thing we need to keep our lives in perspective and our hearts set on the Lord. It helps us refocus our thoughts and actions, and becomes a compass of sorts to keep us headed in the right direction. It keeps us mindful of why we do what we do and who should receive the glory for every good thing. The time we spend in Christian fellowship each week provides a much-needed break from the hectic pace of daily life, so why would we give up such a blessing? Believe it or not, many people do just that.

The Passage:

Read Genesis 2:1-3. Write down key points from the text and journal your thoughts about what you have read:

____

____

____

The Details:

1. What do we learn in Genesis 2:1 about the creation process? Did God leave things unfinished, or was the job complete?

____

____

____

2. When God finished His work, what did He choose to do, according to verse 2?

Which day of the creation story was it? (First, second, etc.)

As we look at this account in Genesis 1 and 2, notice the patterns the Lord establishes. Growth seasons, life cycles, seasons, days, and now a pattern for the cycle of a week. Using God's example, we implement a schedule within our own life of working with our hands, doing the things we need to do, while making sure to set aside a day of rest.

3. God didn't just rest on the seventh day. Look closely at verse three. Why did the Lord designate this day of rest?

God sanctified the seventh day, making it holy. He reflected on the creation He had made. Each Sunday we have the opportunity to stop and reflect on the things of God, and His gift of life.

A Closer Look:

Through the first two chapters of Genesis, we read how God has established the world, the creatures, and in today's lesson, the need for rest. God created the world and all that is in it according to His good pleasure and purpose. The Lord made a point to include a cycle of rest in the creation story, designating the last day as a Sabbath day of blessing and holiness.

The Old Testament believers observed a Sabbath rest on Saturday and the Jewish faith continues to do so today. Most Christians believe that Jesus is the Lord of the Sabbath, and that through His Resurrection, the day of observing the Sabbath shifted to Sunday. Regardless of designation, one day a week is set aside to rejuvenate and worship our Lord. During our day of rest and worship, we are encouraged in the

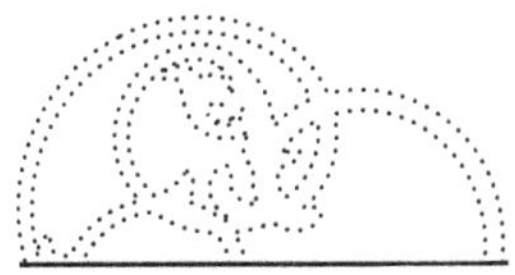

In Genesis 2:3, the Lord blesses and sanctifies the day of rest, making it holy. The Hebrew word for sanctification, *qadash*, stresses that which is holy, sacred or consecrated. God clearly includes a day dedicated to Himself in the creation story.

Word of God, equipped spiritually for the week ahead, and have time to reflect on the majesty of our Lord. He is truly worthy of our praise.

Throughout the Gospels, we read about Jesus setting aside time to rest and pray. Instead of continually serving and working without a break, the Savior modeled the right way to approach the needs and demands we face. A balanced schedule of work, service, rest, and prayer are exemplified in the life of Jesus Christ; our model for living a godly life.

A Question for Your Life Today:

Do you take time to rest each week? Think of your weekly routine, and plan out ways you could implement a Sabbath rest. How would this newly planned rest impact your week?

WORKS CITED:

Baker, Warren and Eugene Carpenter, eds. *The Complete Word Study Dictionary: Old Testament.* Chattanooga: AMG Publishers, 2003:

'Or, #216, p. 27.

Ma'or, #3974, p. 560.

MacArthur, John. *The MacArthur Bible Commentary.* Nashville: Thomas Nelson, Inc, 2005. Pgs 23-24.

WEEK TWO

Righteous God

The Ten Commandments

Exodus 20:1-17

Centuries ago in a land far away, God met Moses on a mountaintop. During that special invitation to worship, Moses received the first inscriptions of Law, etched on stone tablets by the finger of God. Artistic and creative renditions of these two rounded slabs have woven their way into the fabric of our nation's history in a variety of ways. From architectural inclusions in our nation's capitol buildings to yard signs to plaques on the walls of our churches and homes, the commandments are written and displayed with modern translation all over the country.

What relevance do these inscriptions have in our lives today? Are they merely decoration, or do they impact our lives and decisions? Even though the Laws are looked upon with high esteem and respect, all too often they are not given a serious look with regards to life application.

Many people in today's culture will insist that the Ten Commandments are no longer applicable to the church or society for that matter. While we are in the age of grace, we are still accountable to God. The big picture story of the Law is found in Jesus. He summed up the Law. Jesus Christ didn't abolish the Law; He fulfilled it. Our Savior, one third of the Trinity, taught according to the will of the Father and within the story God began at creation. From Genesis to Revelation, God's story points to Jesus Christ and the provision for man's relationship with Him.

This week we will go through the details of the Ten Commandments, giving us a deeper understanding of the familiar words etched on stone thousands of years ago. God's Word is timeless, and He longs for us to live according to His principles. I challenge each of us not only to read the verses, but also to seek the Lord while growing in our obedience to His commands.

The Ten Commandments

No Other Gods	Do Not Murder
No Idols	No Adultery
Honor God's Name	No Stealing
Honor the Sabbath	Do Not Lie
Honor Parents	No Coveting

DAY ONE

NO OTHER GODS, NO IDOLS – EXODUS 20:1-6

The Focus Verse:

You shall have no other gods before Me. **Exodus 20:3**

The Main Thought:

God is the one and only God.

The Story within the Story:

There's nothing more compelling than a good conversion story. From tribal leaders and the demon possessed, to idol worshipers and profit seekers, the Bible is full of amazing stories of people who have heard the message of the gospel and turned from their unbelief. The Bible gives us countless reasons why we can rest assured that no one is *too far* from Jesus' grace and redemption. God was serious when He said "whosoever"!

Take a look at the Apostle Paul. Now there's an unlikely candidate for conversion, yet God said otherwise. In a matter of three days, God totally turned Paul's world upside down and transformed him from a chief persecutor of Christianity to a powerful evangelist ready to travel the region sharing the life-giving message of Jesus Christ. Those we may view as a lost cause, God may view as someone He can use mightily for the kingdom.

The apostle's journeys and writings tell of the impact Paul had in evangelizing many new Christians across the region, such as Lydia the fabric merchant and a nighttime jailer and his family. The apostle was quick to share the good news and faithful to train up new church leadership. Much of the New Testament came from Paul's instruction to churches, disciples, and other believers. What a legacy he left, and he continues to disciple people today through his writings compiled in the Bible.

Missionaries from our generation have some incredible tales to tell of their experiences out in the far reaches of the world, of meeting with the lost and sharing the hope of Jesus Christ, and then watching as the Savior draws more to Himself through the power of His message. When the truth is shared and the hope of salvation is offered to someone who has never heard, the love of Christ can be so overpowering that missionaries have a hard time conveying the magnitude of the moment with mere words in a testimony. Over and over stories surface about conversions happening in the most unlikely environments with the least imaginable characters in some of the harshest circumstances. Yet, the power of God prevails, the Word of the Lord is heard, repentance and confession occur, and a new life in Christ begins.

Sometimes, even when the gospel is heard and Jesus is accepted as Savior, the converts keep their faith hidden because of the fear of death or persecution. A dear friend of mine, a missionary in Africa, tells the tale of secret converts who never audibly profess a faith in God, but meet in secluded places and safe environments to hear the Bible being read, watch evangelistic movies, and learn about Scripture. In their faces, the radiance of belief shines forth, yet in the culture they live in the underground believers' testimonies remain silent. Even in their silence, these new believers understand how precious it is to trust in the God of the Bible. They understand what the cost is to obey this first command; to have no other gods before the almighty God. And, in the dark of night or in the privacy of a safe location, they meet with other Christians to hear the message of the Messiah.

Whether in biblical passages or missionary reports, the powerful accounts of new believers impact our lives in so many ways. They show us the transformational power of the Word of God. They reveal the need for the truth in lives filled with spiritual darkness. Testimonies should move our hearts with compassion and help us take intentional steps towards spreading the good news of salvation in our own spheres of influence. Why? Because the first commandment tells us to love God only. Those who do not have a relationship with the Lord and think that being *good* is enough will never know the love of Christ. We must love God. As we love God, we will be compelled to share His love with others.

The Passage:

Read Exodus 20:1-6. Write down key points from the text and journal your thoughts about what you have read:

The Details:

1. Read Exodus 20:1-2. What did God remind the people of concerning their history?

It intrigues me that the Lord reminds the people how He has provided for them and how he released them from captivity before He shares His commands. As God makes covenant with His people, He affirms that He loved them first. Before He outlines the rules requiring obedience, He has already blessed them. The commands are established to keep the Israelites living in blessing. As we remain in the Lord's will for our lives, we also will be blessed.

2. In verse 3, God gives the first commandment for His people to follow. What is it?

Why do you think this commandment came first? Describe why God used this first Law to lay a foundation for the rest of the commands.

Before any other Law, God establishes the fact that He is the one God over all. He is the focus of their worship. He is the provider of life, and the highest authority in their lives. As a foundation to all the commands to follow, the Lord reinforces the value of obedience and focused faith.

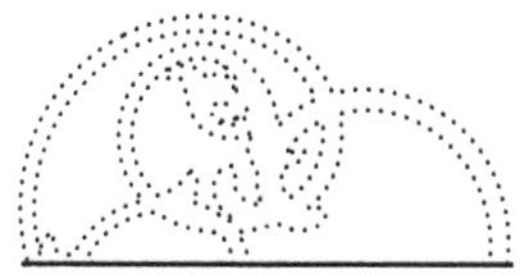

"You shall not make *other gods* besides Me; gods of silver or gods of gold, you shall not make for yourselves."

Exodus 20:23 [*Emphasis added.*]

3. Look at Exodus 20:4. Now that the Lord has established that He is the one true God, what is His next command for His people?

4. Not only are they not to make idols, verse five tells us they are not to ____________ ____________ them or ____________________ them. Why? (Verses 5 and 6)

An idol is anything that is more important to us than God.

God's people are clearly told not to *make, worship,* or *serve* idols. While we may think we are immune to the lures of idolatry, let's think about what constitutes an idol. An idol can be a graven image, but it can also mean *anything* we place in higher importance than the Lord. With that in mind, what are some "idols" in our culture and lives today? Journal your thoughts:

A Closer Look:

Idolatry can take many forms, and can sneak in when we least expect it. A desire for the nicer things in life, if left unchecked, can grow into a lifestyle of greed and materialism. Physical training taken to an unhealthy obsession can become an idol of self worship. Climbing the corporate ladder and forgetting the Lord in the process builds the idol of pride, power, and greed.

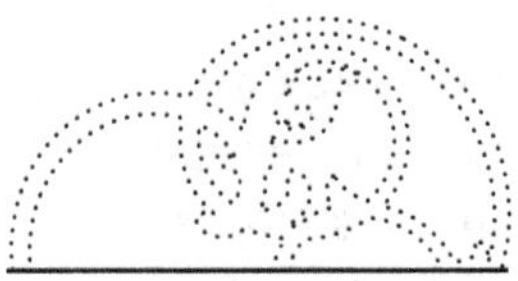

"To whom then will you liken God? Or what likeness will you compare with Him?"

Isaiah 40:18

With God as our focus of worship, the areas in our lives that have the potential to become idols to us will remain in balance. The first two commandments reaffirm the fact that the God of the Bible is our Creator. He is the one true God and He will not be given second place to anything else in creation. He knows who He is, and who we are—with and without Him. He longs for us to worship and serve Him. God created us to love and enjoy Him!

A Question for Your Life Today:

Think about your childhood. Did you learn the Ten Commandments? How did that knowledge shape your choices and decisions as a child?

DAY TWO

HONOR GOD'S NAME, HONOR THE SABBATH – EXODUS 20:7-11

The Focus Verse:

Remember the sabbath day, to keep it holy. **Exodus 20:8**

The Main Thought:

Honor God's name, keep His day holy.

The Story within the Story:

We can learn a lot about love by listening to the conversations in the school yard during recess. Picture the usual recess scene: kids running everywhere, playground castles full of busy bodies and chatting mouths, and personalities clashing with each passing of the swings on the swing set. While the children in the middle of a disagreement will talk back to anyone who throws an insult, there is an invisible line in the playground gravel. Nobody can get away with disrespecting family. *Mess with me, but don't talk bad about my momma.*

Remember the days? Trouble abounds and then someone starts in with, "Your momma's so . . ." and from there, the next world war erupts. Words fly faster than bees buzzing around the dumpsters. Kids form a circle and take ringside seats. That line, when crossed, evokes a response unlike any other. Why? We love our parents. We love our moms, and we want to make sure they are respected.

Do we give the Lord the same level of respect? More respect? The Ten Commandments clearly instruct that we should. We will discover that God states that all who take His name lightly (or in vain) will be punished. He takes respect and authority seriously, and as a people who love God, we are to worship Him with reverence and awe.

As we respect the Lord's name, we are also called to set aside time to worship Him. God gives us the opportunity to take a "time out" from the craziness of life to rest, reflect on His goodness, and refuel spiritually before the next work week begins. God didn't call for a Sabbath rest so we could run more errands; He established it as a remembrance of His work in Creation, and His relationship with us. Let us honor the Lord through respect and worship.

The Passage:

Read Exodus 20:7-11. Write down key points from the text and journal your thoughts about what you have read:

The Details:

1. Exodus 20:7 gives us the third commandment. What is it?

____

____

____

What is the consequence of breaking this command, according to the second half of verse seven?

____

____

____

We learn that the Lord will punish whoever takes His name in vain. *The Complete Word Study Dictionary: Old Testament* tells us that the phrase "in vain" translated from the Hebrew term *saw'* "is used to describe what is prohibited" (p. 1107). Other uses of this world indicate lying, useless activities, and worthless efforts. When we take the Lord's name in vain, which is prohibited, we are participating in an evil act of no value. Simply, we are not valuing the name of God.

This definition gives us a clearer insight into the magnitude of this command. God isn't just looking for the easy checklist response (not swearing falsely); He wants us to live with reverential, holy fear of the almighty God we serve. We cannot take Him or His ways lightly, and cannot discount the majesty of His role as Creator.

2. Write out the next commandment, found in verse eight:

____

____

____

____

3. Verses nine and ten give us more insight on why we have this command. What do these verses reveal?

4. Read Exodus 31:12-18. What does the Lord tell Moses about the Sabbath in this passage?

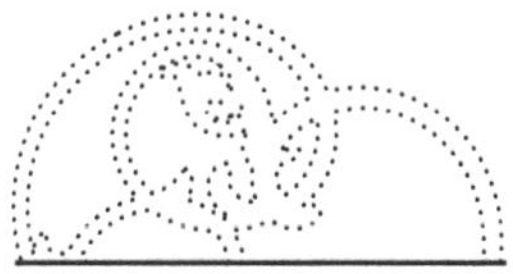

"...that you may know that I am the LORD who sanctifies you."

Exodus 31:13

5. What does God remind us of in Exodus 20:11? What is the association between our Sabbath and the seventh day of creation?

Just as the first Sabbath, on the seventh day of creation, was a time of refreshing for the Lord, the Sabbath rest for us is designed by God to equip us with strength for the week ahead of us. God consecrated the Sabbath, made it holy, as a sign that He is the One who also sanctifies us, or makes us more holy through our relationship with Him.

A Closer Look:

Respecting God and not blaspheming His Name are ways we show our love for the Lord. Living holy lives hinges on reverencing the God we serve. Observing a day of rest, as established by God Himself, is another integral way of exhibiting our love and respect for our Lord. The first four commands all focus on making God the object of our worship and living a life that reflects our commitment to God; heart, mind, soul, and strength.

A Question for Your Life Today:

As we have looked into these commandments, and have seen that the first four deal with God and our uncompromising faith in Him, let's think about the compromise in today's culture. According to the first four commandments, how does God feel about the popular profession that "all paths lead to heaven" or "all gods are the same"?

DAY THREE

HONOR LIFE – EXODUS 20:12-13

The Focus Verse:

You shall not murder. **Exodus 20:13**

The Main Thought:

Honor the gift of life.

The Story within the Story:

The witnesses' robes were thrown to the dusty ground, landing at the religious leaders' feet. The crowd circled the target, collected stones in hand, and took aim. The life of an innocent man was extinguished in the midst of zealous persecution. The story of Stephen's death is just that simple; that graphic. And Saul saw the whole thing. He approved it. In Acts 8:1, we find that "Saul was in hearty agreement with putting him to death." *Present and guilty.* He watched the murder take place, and didn't do a thing about it.

How could this happen? How could Saul be so hardened that he set his heart on seeking out followers of Jesus in order to take them captive or to take their lives? The religious leader knew the Law; he had been trained by Gamaliel, a prominent religious teacher. Saul understood the command, "Do not murder," yet in a quest to keep the truth of Jesus quiet, the command to respect life was ignored. Somewhere along the line, respect for human life disappeared from the conscience of young Saul. But Saul isn't the only person in history guilty of such hardening of the heart. In the past and in our lives today, murder, even by religious motive, is still murder.

Cain, in a jealous moment of anger against his brother, became the first recorded murderer in the Bible. Even Moses, the one whom the Lord trusted with the first tablets on the mountaintop, killed an Egyptian out of a rage birthed from a protective spirit for his people. Later, those who knew the Ten Commandments seemed to overlook the inconvenient truths of God when their own wisdom prevailed as seen with David. The man after God's own heart, David, committed the sin of coveting another's wife. He committed adultery, bore false witness, and murdered her husband, all in an impulsive season of bad decisions regarding Bathsheba.

What can we learn from all the examples God has given us in the Scriptures? Murder, no matter the motive, is still sin. It grieves the heart of God. It's the difference between honoring and disrespecting the value of life.

The Passage:

Read Exodus 20:12-13. Write down key points from the text and journal your thoughts about what you have read:

____

____

____

The Details:

1. What does Exodus 20:12 tell us about honoring our parents? What benefits do we receive for honoring them?

____

____

____

"For the husband is the head of the wife, as Christ also is the head of the church, He Himself *being* the Savior of the body."

Ephesians 5:23 [*Emphasis added.*]

It is interesting to note that the first commandment that deals with our relationships with others involves our parents. This commandment is also the first that contains a promise. As we honor our parents, the Lord promises to prolong our days. In order to be a family that honors the Lord, we must honor the structure within our own household. The two go hand in hand; we interact with others much like we interact with God. The family structure is close to the structure we have in the church. Just as Christ is the head of the church, the father is the head of the home.

Record Leviticus 19:3:

____

____

____

In this verse, we see the principles of the fourth commandment repeated. The term *reverence* is interchanged with the word *honor* in this verse. The Hebrew word for reverence, *yare*, refers to having a "holy respect" for your parents. After the first four commands, God is showing the consistency of His requirements as they translate to our daily lives and interactions with others. The overflow of our love for God will be shown in our love for others.

How does this command impact your own life? Have you ever struggled with honoring your parents? If you have children, do you experience times where you do not feel you are respected by them? Journal your thoughts:

____

____

____

Take a moment to pray, asking the Lord to forgive you for times when you have been disrespectful. Ask God to give your children a desire to honor you and your spouse. Commit your families to the Lord.

2. What is the next commandment, listed in verse 13?

____

____

____

This type of murder, premeditated and planned out, has severe consequences according to the Word of God. Cities of refuge were established so that people who had killed another person accidentally could seek asylum; but for those who planned murder, there was no provision for asylum. God is clear in His anger against those who take another's life.

The love of God is present even in the midst of His anger. The Lord longs for the lost to repent and accept Jesus' sacrifice. He desires relationship with all His children. The gift of salvation is available to all who repent and believe; even murderers. I've heard stories of death row inmates who have repented and accepted Jesus as Savior shortly before their death. When sin is cleansed, it is forgotten. *Gone.*

Can you think of a time when you were angry enough to even think about harming another person? Do you see how respect for human life and your belief in Christian principles keep you balanced, and restrain you from making a terrible mistake?

____

____

____

Pause and praise God for His love for you. Thank the Holy Spirit for guiding you into right choices. Even in our most angry or frustrated moments, taking another's life cannot be justified. Life, given by God, is designed to glorify Him.

A Closer Look:

Our own parents were gracious enough to give us life and raise us until we were independent enough to make it on our own. We are living proof of our parents' respect for life. When we began growing in our mother's wombs, preparations began for providing for our needs; first with diapers and bottles, then with meals, soccer gear, and school supplies. Our mothers and fathers have modeled for us what it means to care for another life. Respecting our parents deals with respecting the gift of the life they gave us and the role they have as our caretakers. Parents model a respect for life, and teach us how to live according to God's Laws.

We see this week that on the heels of the command to honor our parents comes a command to honor the lives of others by not murdering. This commandment is easy to obey if we have a respect for life. Why would we kill someone if we understand they are special in God's eye? When we respect the value of the lives around us we will never consider murder.

A Question for Your Life Today:

How does this week's focus on the commandments change your outlook on the many gods (polytheistic) environment we live in?

DAY FOUR

NO ADULTERY, NO STEALING – EXODUS 20:14-15

The Focus Verse:

You shall not steal. **Exodus 20:15**

The Main Thought:

Don't take what doesn't belong to you!

The Story within the Story:

I have recently noticed a very peculiar television show. The entire purpose of the half-hour segments revolves around a camera crew catching people in the throws of adultery. The viewers witness film clips of secret couples walking through parking lots, eating at restaurants, and driving in cars. Such proof of external relationships reveals the guilty partner's indiscretions, as the sinners are tracked by the show's producers. Before each program ends, the confrontation between the innocent victim and the guilty cheater is aired on national TV with as much compassion as the nightly news.

What happens to these families? What benefit is there to having such sin broadcast from state to state? While this method may be effective in exposing the sin, I'm not sure how much it truly benefits the innocent person who watches his or her loved one running around town in the game of secret sin. Adultery ruins lives.

Watching the daily news programs, we are bound to witness reports of crooks stealing equipment, consumer goods, cash or cars. Stories of court room cases, high speed car chases, and prison sentences fill our newspapers. Crime doesn't pay and those who don't want to pay for the items have two options: do without, or pay the price of stealing and getting caught. Those who don't get caught stealing will usually continue in the destructive pattern until they are finally apprehended. Sin left unchecked leads to further sin.

Today's lesson deals with two commandments: adultery and stealing. On the surface there is quite a parallel between the two commands. One steals a person's loved one, the other steals objects or items of value. The root of both sins stems from a sense that the person's life is missing something. This perceived lack leads the sinner to find comfort in people or items that belong to someone else. This can become a vivid example of those who believe the phrase, "the grass is greener on the other side of the fence." Most times, when people finally get to that other patch of grass, they find it was really not as green as they expected. Sin never fully satisfies.

The Passage:

Read Exodus 20:14-15. Write down key points from the text and journal your thoughts about what you have read:

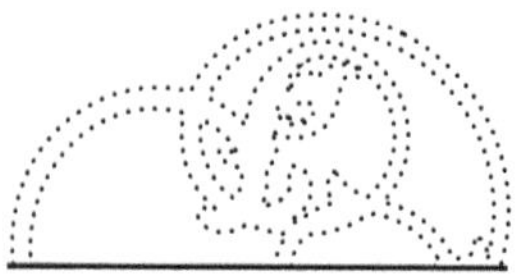

"For this reason a man shall leave his father and his mother, and be joined to his wife; and they shall become one flesh."

Genesis 2:24

The Details:

1. What impact, if any, has adultery had on your life or the lives of those you know? Have you seen others hurt by an adulterous relationship?

____

____

____

2. Why do you think God included this command in the list?

Just as God commands that we obey Him and serve Him only, He also calls us to be faithful in our earthly relationships. Honoring our parents and the lives of others is critical, as is the respect of our spouse and marriage commitment.

3. Exodus 20:15 gives another simple yet important command. What is it?

____

____

____

Have you ever been tempted to steal something? What was the result of your sin? Were you caught, and did you return the item?

____

____

____

Can you imagine God's response when we steal? What do you think God's motive is for putting this command in the same category as murder and idolatry?

____

____

____

____

We serve a God who loves to bless us with good things and loving relationships. As Christians, we are not to seek temporal gain or worldly wealth. Through the Father's love for us, we are shown how to love others with a true and honest love. As believers, we are admonished to live within the principles of the Lord. God is grieved when we aren't content with what we have and the blessings He has given us. To want what others have and steal what isn't ours circumvents God's will for us and His plan for our lives.

A Closer Look:

There's quite a theme to the commands we are studying this week. Putting God first in our life and respecting the lives of others around us will lead to a life based on truth, honor, and integrity. An upright, blameless life is a blessed life. As we love God and love others, we also learn to be content with what we have; not seeking to steal, kill or destroy what belongs to someone else. In John 10:10, Jesus tells us that "The thief comes only to steal and kill and destroy; I came that they may have life, and might have *it* abundantly." [*Emphasis added.*] May we live abundant lives in Jesus Christ!

A Question for Your Life Today:

What would you say to someone who asked you about the God of the Bible, and whether He is equal to the gods of other faiths?

DAY FIVE

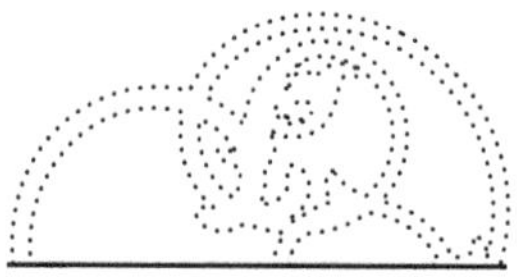

Competing with the wealth and lifestyle of others leads to selfish ambition, coveting, and distraction.

NO FALSE WITNESS, NO COVETING – EXODUS 20:16-17

The Focus Verse:

You shall not bear false witness against your neighbor. **Exodus 20:16**

The Main Thought:

Love your neighbors.

The Story within the Story:

Keeping up with the Joneses. We've all seen it. We've probably all tried it at some point in life. Just like the household vacuum cleaner pulling dirt into the canister with a force the debris can't resist, the temptation to compete with others for consumer goods, status, or prestige can suck us in before we realize what has happened. Suddenly, we may find ourselves leading a lifestyle we never imagined, or climbing out of a mountain of debt we can't believe we accumulated.

Competing with neighbors for the best technology, nicest car, and most perfect kids can be down right tiring. Who has time to keep track of the neighbor's newest purchase in today's busy world? Unfortunately, that trap of competition catches far too many people. Through trusting the Lord, obeying His commands, and cultivating humble hearts, we can avoid the temptation to want things just because others have them. Impure motives are birthed out of a heart that isn't focused on the Lord. By obeying God's command and design for our lives, we are better equipped to steer clear of the traps of coveting and competing.

What are the priorities God sets for us? What are the goals He has for our lives? I can guarantee that the Lord isn't concerned with comparing our car with the car our neighbor drives. God is concerned with our personal relationship with Him, and how we honor Him in our actions and interactions with others. So while we are called to love our neighbors, we are not called to compete with their worldly reputations, goods, and possessions.

The Passage:

Read Exodus 20:16-17. Write down key points from the text and journal your thoughts about what you have read:

The Details:

1. What does Exodus 20:16 tell us? Record the verse:

2. What is your reaction to such a command? What does "bear false witness" mean to you?

The Hebrew term for "bear false witness" is *seqer*, a word that refers to a lie or something fraudulent. *The Complete Word Study Dictionary: Old Testament* explains this term *seqer* as "a lie, vanity, without cause" (p.1195).

3. Is this mention of "neighbor" limited to the person who lives next to you? Who else does the term "neighbor" refer to?

____

____

____

4. As an extension of the ninth commandment, the tenth expands on our relationship with our neighbor. Along with the command to not bear false witness, what does verse 17 tell us we are to refrain from doing?

____

____

____

As we see with these last two commands, honoring our neighbor means interacting with honesty and respect. Verse 17 clearly teaches us that we shouldn't covet the possessions of others; whether servants, resources, animals, or family members. "Covet," *hamad* in Hebrew, refers to longing for, lusting, or craving with a fleshly, uncontrollable desire. This is more than simply admiring an item and thinking it would be nice to have—coveting is more of a compulsory obsession for something just out of reach. Coveting can be thought of as a stepping stone to lying, adultery, stealing, and even murder. What begins with a feeling of discontent in any area of our lives can grow into a life of sin.

A Closer Look:

Through our journey this week, we have studied the commands that Moses received from God. Paul tells us in Galatians 3:24 that, "The Law has become our tutor to lead us to Christ, so that we may be justified by faith." What began with the covenant between God and Abraham, continued with the Law given to Moses, and became fulfilled with the coming of the Messiah. Jesus, the Son of God, came to fulfill the Law, not abolish it.

During Jesus' ministry on earth, interesting questions about the Law began to surface. Was it still relevant? Did the Law have a place in the ministry of Jesus Christ? While Jesus taught about love, He also clearly taught about staying within the will of the Father. Nevertheless, questions arose from seekers and religious leaders alike.

In the gospels we have a record of a moment when the religious leaders and scribes approached Jesus with obscure questions in an attempt to trap Him with His own words. One question in the interrogator's lineup rallied around which command was the greatest. What began with a conversational trap became a wonderful teaching tool by the Son of God. Jesus addressed the issue of the Ten Commandments in a simple and powerful way. The Messiah's answer was clear: "Love God; love others." All ten commands were summed up in two. Mark 12:29-31 records His response this way:

> "The foremost is, 'HEAR, O ISRAEL! THE LORD OUR GOD IS ONE LORD; AND YOU SHALL LOVE THE LORD YOUR GOD WITH ALL YOUR HEART, AND WITH ALL YOUR SOUL, AND WITH ALL YOUR MIND, AND WITH ALL YOUR STRENGTH.' The second is this, 'YOU SHALL LOVE YOUR NEIGHBOR AS YOURSELF.' There is no other commandment greater than these."

The Savior's instruction does not negate any of the original commands given to Moses. Jesus simply condensed the ten laws from the tablets into an overall lifestyle that surpasses the details of the ten and leads to a life committed to living for God. The summation went straight for the *fruit* of the believer—for the lifestyle that would result from serving God in complete surrender and obedience. Jesus clearly taught the need for obeying God as shown in His statement in John 14:15: "If you love Me, you will keep My commandments." Love and obedience to God go hand in hand.

By focusing on loving God and loving others, the Ten Commandments will be obeyed and a godly lifestyle will be displayed through our daily actions. As we seek Jesus and obediently follow Him, our love will increase with each passing day. The Ten Commandments will no longer be viewed as a set of rules that seem out of reach; they will become a framework that our lives exemplify as we live in ways that reflect the Savior.

A Question for Your Life Today:

This week we have looked at how to honor and love God, and how to respect and love others. Think about your relationships for a moment. How does your relationship with God impact the relationships you have with others? Does your spiritual relationship impact your natural relationships?

WORKS CITED:

Baker, Warren and Eugene Carpenter, eds. *The Complete Word Study Dictionary: Old Testament.* Chattanooga: AMG Publishers, 2003:

Saw, #7723, p. 1107.

Seqer, #8267, p. 1195.

Hamad, #2530, p. 348.

WEEK THREE

All Wise God

Trust in the Lord

Proverbs 3:5-6

Flying into Texas airspace, making our final descent toward the military airstrip, it was impossible to fully fathom what the next two weeks would include. All I could focus on was the reality of our long flight cooped up in that military aircraft while traveling from Panama to the US for special medical treatment. Tests, more tests, travel, surgery, and tons of prayer were waiting us upon landing. My baby was going to undergo heart surgery and I was totally at the mercy of God, the skill of the doctors, and the beat of my little boy's heart.

The hole in his heart needed immediate attention requiring delicate surgery. At 18 months, his heart muscle had pumped as many times as a six-year-old's heart. His hole required a patch, a vein required a shunt, and we needed a boost of faith to get us through each moment of fear and worry. It is at those very moments that we had a decision to make; choose to let our worries take over and destroy us, or choose to let God be Lord of our lives in to a depth we had never experienced. *We chose God.*

With a constant trust in God, our family stepped through each stressful decision and procedure with an underlying confidence that the Lord was with us and that His wisdom far outweighed ours. We acknowledged that He was in control and calling the shots. Praise God we weren't totally dependant on earthly wisdom!

God's wisdom far surpasses human logic. Two weeks, a procedure, and later a transfer to Washington DC for surgery and a hospital stay. We watched our son speed down the road to recovery. Things worked out incredibly well, and we give God the glory for each moment of triumph.

Looking back on that journey, I am thankful for the ways the Lord stood with us and provided when we didn't even realize how much we needed provision. He loved us when we desperately needed love and support. That traumatic season of medical crisis brought with it spiritual growth that will stay with us a lifetime. It taught us that as we learn more about the Lord and grow in our relationship with Him, those new levels of spiritual maturity remain and support us in future need.

Trusting in the Lord is so much more than memorizing a quick verse. Our life experiences and struggles shape how we respond to adversity, and the Lord uses each and every moment of our lives to cultivate trust and love in our hearts; transforming us into the image of a Christ follower. Truly, may we lean not on our own wisdom, but may we rise up and confidently rely on wisdom from above. As James so clearly instructs, "Wisdom from above is first pure, then peaceable, gentle, full of mercy and good fruits, unwavering, without hypocrisy" (James 3:17). Through this chapter, we will learn more about the entire third chapter of Proverbs and how trusting in the Lord is an integral part of following Him.

DAY ONE

KEEP YOUR HEART SET ON GOD – PROVERBS 3:1-4

The Focus Verse:

Do not forget my teaching, but let your heart keep my commandments. **Proverbs 3:1**

The Main Thought:

Love God.

The Story within the Story:

Although the root of the problem is different, our son's need for a repaired heart reminds me of the spiritual heart renewal we experience through conversion. Because of the sin of Adam and Eve, mankind needs the atoning sacrifice only God can provide. That sacrifice, fulfilled once and for all through the shedding of Jesus' blood at Calvary, makes it possible for our hearts to be mended with God; if we choose to receive Jesus' gift of salvation. In the same way that we had to actively ask for surgery for a little boy, we have to repent of our sins and ask the Lord for His gift of redemption.

Through our status as believers, we become a new creation, with a "heart transplant," of sorts, that gives us a desire and longing to know God more fully each day. A Christian's new heart is not a supplementary organ surgically placed in the body. It is the Spirit of the Living God dwelling in us through conversion and the conduit through which our innermost being, or spirit, relates to the Lord. This relationship is thought of as our "heart"—the essence, core, and most private recesses of our lives.

Jesus tells us that the role of the Holy Spirit in the lives of believers is to "teach you all things, and bring to your remembrance all that I said to you" (John 14:26). The Holy Spirit is our Helper, our Counselor, and the One who guides us into right decisions. The seven-fold Spirit of God brings wisdom to all who believe that Jesus is the Son of God. It is through our relationship with the Father and the Son that this wisdom from the Spirit is given.

As we allow God to rule our lives, the process for making choices changes. What we view as a "smart thing to do" may shift. Our own wisdom will no longer prevail and God's direction and guidance will begin to shape our decisions. His design for our lives will become the priority and the Holy Spirit will lead our decisions.

The Passage:

Read Proverbs 3:1-4. Write down key points from the text and journal your thoughts about what you have read:

The Details:

1. Where should we "keep" God's commandments?

____

____

____

The heart, mentioned in this passage, refers to our innermost being—our inner spirit. It is in this area that we have relationship with the Lord.

2. What is the benefit of keeping God's commands, according to verse 2?

____

____

____

Through our desire to obey God's commands, we will enjoy a long, peaceful life. While God does not promise a life without problems, He does say that He will be faithful to come alongside and give us peace; no matter what we might be facing. Just as our son's heart surgery has prolonged his life significantly, our new heart as a believer brings us prolonged life on earth–as well as eternal life in heaven.

The Hebrew word *hesed*, or "lovingkindness," is translated in verse 3 as "mercy," "love," or "kindness." Coupled with truth or faithfulness, we can think of this type of mercy stemming from the character and love of God; the unconditional love that comes through the Savior.

3. In verse 3, what does God tell us to hold on to?

____________________ and ____________________

We are instructed to not allow *kindness* [the NASB version says kindness] (*or love or mercy*) and *truth* (*or faithfulness*) to leave us by binding them ______________ our ______________ and writing them on the ______________ of our ______________.

In these first few verses, we learn that keeping God's commands close to us means more than memorizing a few words or hanging a plaque on a wall. Our relationship with God is cultivated and grown in our heart; our spirit. The result of this spiritual growth is explained in Proverbs 3:4. What does this verse reveal about the benefits of obeying God's commands?

Staying close to the Lord and growing in the Word brings favor and good repute, or understanding. The Lord blesses those who seek Him and follow His guidelines. As the Holman Christian Standard Bible puts it; we will "find favor and high regard in the sight of God and man" (Proverbs 3:4).

"Repute," high regard or understanding, comes from the Hebrew term *sekhel*, which means happiness or success and understanding. Our wisdom for life when based on the Bible brings forth positive results to our lives. God longs to bless those who follow Him.

A Closer Look:

Our reputation with God is more critical than our relationship with any person. As we obey His commands and apply His truth to our lives, we stand before God with a good reputation and with favor. The lovingkindness that can only come from the Almighty God is more abundant than anything we can imagine.

It is one thing to show love, and another to be kind. Any human can cultivate the qualities of love and kindness. But the lovingkindness of the Lord far surpasses the most loving moment or kindest act here on earth. He has provided for our eternal victory over the grave and He wants to see us live our lives with blessing and honor as we give Him glory for all things.

Matthew records the description of God's blessings by the Messiah's own words:

What man is there among you, when his son asks for a loaf, will give him a stone? Or if he asks for a fish, he will not give him a snake, will he? If you then, being evil, know how to give good gifts to your children, how much more will your Father who is in heaven give what is good to those who ask Him! (Matthew 7:9-11).

But look closer at our passage in Proverbs. Not only will we find favor with God, we are also given good reputation "with man." While the favor of man is enjoyed by the godly, the converse is not always true. Finding favor with man doesn't instantly guarantee favor with God, yet true blessing and complete favor comes from one source: the God of the Bible.

A Question for Your Life Today:

Think about the issues and life choices you are facing today. In those areas of your life, are you putting your trust in God for direction and wisdom?

DAY TWO

THE SOUND BYTE EXPLORED – PROVERBS 3:5-6

The Focus Verse:

Trust in the Lord with all your heart and do not lean on your own understanding. **Proverbs 3:5**

The Main Thought:

Trust God.

The Story within the Story:

Over the past few years, I've tracked this particular set of popular verses (Proverbs 3:5-6) through a maze of trendy uses. A favorite saying for bookmarks, gift items, and artwork, "leaning not on our own understanding" has become a predictable household phrase. Unfortunately, as these verses have been set on a pedestal of convenient quips from the Word, they fall prey to the danger of losing their luster while in the limelight.

From public speeches to chapel services to somebody's "life verse," Proverbs 3:5-6 has become a buzz passage that is recited with ease and affirmed by crowds in nods of empathy. Like any other well-used sound-byte, the words have become more than predictable; and have begun to mean less than what God intended. God's Word never returns void and God's Word is always true, but does the person who quotes the verse understand the magnitude of this truth? We have many opportunities each day to rely on our own wisdom, or choose to rely on God's truth.

This set of verses, tucked into the book of Proverbs, has become a rallying point to many—even unbelievers. I've heard this verse spoken with affirmation by New Age followers who ascribe this wisdom of God to a false "god" of their imaginations. Non-Christians may easily agree with the words we speak, but if they are not in agreement with a belief in the God of Abraham, Isaac, and Jacob, true godly wisdom escapes them. Unless they exclusively worship the one true God of the Bible, there is no connection with the wisdom of the Father and the wisdom they rely on.

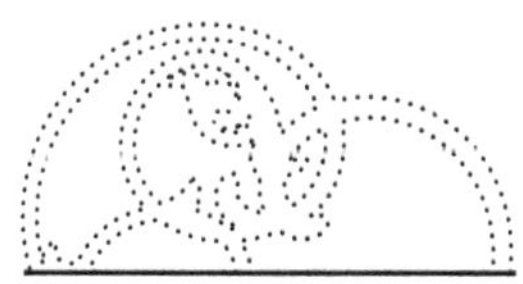

Do we realize the power of the words we quote with ease?

Do we realize the power of the words we quote with ease? Do we tell the story of the life lessons and struggles that have caused us to quote the words of verses five and six? When we need direction, guidance, and a straight path, do we quickly heed these words, or just speak them out as we would speak out our drive-thru order?

Truly, we must lean on the Lord and trust His direction--not only when we are in the middle of an unusual crisis, but every day and in every moment of our lives. The source of godly wisdom is God. He longs for His people to call upon Him, humble themselves, and follow His lead. As we acknowledge God and allow Him to be Lord of our lives, things will change. Our life story will reflect the Father's commands. Our wise choices will become a little wiser in the eyes of God.

The Passage:

Read Proverbs 3:5-6. Write down key points from the text and journal your thoughts about what you have read:

The Details:

1. Fill in Proverbs 3:5-6:

" ____________________ in the ____________________ with all
your ____________________ and do not ____________________
on your own ____ . In
____________________ your ways ____________________ Him, and
________ will make your paths ____________________ ."

Trust God, and He will keep you on the right path. Lean on His understanding, not yours, for wise decisions in life. Acknowledge God and give Him the glory for every good thing. Praise the Lord in all circumstances!

2. Read Jeremiah 9:23-24. What are we told not to boast about? (v.23)

____

____

____

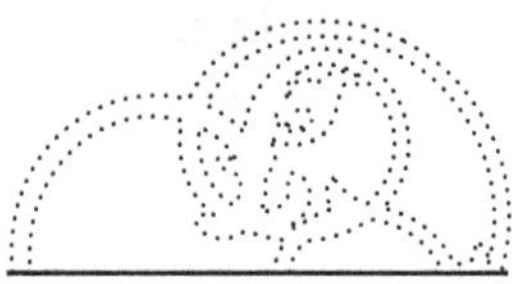

"'But let him who boasts boast of this, that he understands and knows Me, that I am the LORD who exercises lovingkindness, justice and righteousness on earth; for I delight in these things,' declares the Lord."

Jeremiah 9:24

In verse 24, what are we encouraged to boast about? What new insight do we gain about God's ways?

____

____

____

God doesn't want us to boast about our own wisdom, riches or might; He is looking for followers who will boast about who God is, and how He blesses our lives.

3. Have you relied on Proverbs 3:5-6, or heard it quoted? ____________________

Does this study session shed new light on the depth of the quote? ____________________

How would you explain this passage to others if they used it in a trite way?

4. Think of a struggle or difficult time in your life. Did you trust in God during that time? Did you lean on His guidance or did you implement your wisdom and plan? What was the outcome? Journal about the experience you just thought through. Then think about how increasing your dependence on God would help with future issues.

A Closer Look:

Unlike the Hebrew term *sekel* used in verse four, the translation of "understanding" in verse five is *binyah*, which refers to "intelligence" and "insight." As we see with Proverbs 3:5, we are warned against relying on our own wisdom and intelligence. We are encouraged to look to God for guidance and direction.

Sounds easy enough, but do our lives reflect such a leaning? All too often, when we are caught in a pinch, God's best is pushed aside as we lean on our own logic. Instead of walking on the safe path of all God has for us, we step into the ditch of human limitations.

Why do we so easily give up God's best for us? In our haste to follow our own lead, we forego the blessings of God as easily as we overlook a shiny new penny on the sidewalk. Whether a coin at our feet or God's best at our fingertips, we may not realize why it is worth stopping and taking hold of what is offered. As God reveals His plan for our lives, we may question whether the little blessing in front of us is worth our precious time, and we wonder if it fits in with *our* plans for the day.

Oh how the Lord's plans are not our plans. Oh how His ways are not our ways. Our best laid plans pale in comparison to the blessings the Lord has for His children. His heart is full of love for His people and He longs to bless the body of believers . . . but are we willing to follow His lead, and obediently go where He tells us to go?

A Question for Your Life Today:

In what areas of your life do you need to trust God more? Describe them and how you can implement new ways to lean on God in those areas:

____

____

____

____

DAY THREE

GOD'S WISDOM, OUR TREASURE – PROVERBS 3:7-18

The Focus Verse:

How blessed is the man who finds wisdom and the man who gains understanding. **Proverbs 3:13**

The Main Thought:

God blesses you as you trust Him.

The Story within the Story:

A friend once told me a story that exemplifies what can go wrong when we use our own wisdom. The tale involves the mischievous antics of her two sons who thought it would be fun to play with the garden hose. On this particularly beautiful summer day, the boys went out to the yard, grabbed the hose, turned on the faucet, and squealed with glee as the water arched out of the end of the tube. They soon tired of playing alone on the front lawn and wanted to think up a new game. Before long the plan was hatched and they excitedly ran full speed ahead into a trap of unsound decisions.

In their three- and five-year -old wisdom, the boys decided to help Mom clean house. They had helped her use the mop before and knew it took a bucket of water to do the job right. Sure, she had told them not to try stuff like this on their own. Of course, Mom had set boundaries and been clear about keeping the hose outside. No doubt the boys knew the rules, but somehow, in this moment of massive creativity, they threw caution to the wind and opted for preschool smarts to guide them. And, they had the hose in their hands.

As the water spewed out of the tube, they realized what a perfect source for water it was. With such realization, they were set for the next phase of their special operation. Instead of a bucket, the boys opted for the mentality, "What a little will do, a lot will do better." No need for a bucket when you've got a constant water supply. Trouble was really starting to brew.

As the younger son opened the front door, the older child held the hose, and together, they entered the foyer hallway. Water flowed freely from the hose with each step. *Spill, splash, gurgle, drench* just as they planned. The water quickly filled up the hallway and seeped into the living room. The boys were bubbling over with excitement as they imagined how that tile floor would sparkle when it was clean! In their minds they would be receiving plenty of accolades, and hopefully, cookies too, for a job well done. The rules they had been given paled in comparison to the brilliant plan they had just conceived. And the tile was looking so shiny!

You can imagine the scene as Mom found her house being ruined by a spraying garden hose. She ran down the stairs, surveyed the water damage in places that had never seen water, and floors ankle deep in a river of good intentions. She locked eyes with her angelically mischievous boys who were grinning ear to ear with satisfaction. You can guess the rest of the story. No cookies, lots of cleaning, and two angels spending lots of time in their rooms. How can wisdom in one mind be such foolishness in another's mind? Easy. Just ask the mom.

Just as those children did what made sense to them, believers in all generations have made the mistake of relying on personal wisdom instead of the truth of the Bible. If we *live* by the wisdom of God, our lives will *reflect* the wisdom of God. Our choices and priorities will reveal what we truly trust. Hopefully, as a people who know the rules, God won't catch us standing in the hallway with a hose and a grin . . . doing the last thing He ever thought we'd do.

If we *live* by the wisdom of God, our lives will *reflect* the wisdom of God.

The Passage:

Read Proverbs 3:7-18. Write down key points from the text and journal your thoughts about what you have read:

____

____

____

The Details:

1. What admonishment is given in verse 7a?

____

____

____

The Hebrew term for "wise," *hakam*, also refers to being clever or prudent. As with our story of the boys and the garden hose, they were definitely "wise in their own eyes." What is wisdom to one may be complete foolishness to another.

What is the instruction given in the second portion Proverbs 3:7?

____

____

____

Not only are we told to value God's wisdom, we also learn that we are to turn away from evil and have a holy respect, or fear, for the Lord. These two concepts truly go hand in hand. As we fear the Lord, we will honor His wisdom over ours.

2. What is the benefit of fearing the Lord, according to verse 8?

____

____

A healthy body and nourishment to our bones! What a wonderful promise! Trusting in the Lord takes away the stress of relying on ourselves. Times of refreshing come from the Lord, and as we allow Him to be our source of wisdom, we will be more peaceful and healthy.

3. What is the focus of verses 9 and 10?

What is the benefit of honoring God with our wealth?

As we give tithes and offerings to the Lord, sharing the first fruits or first portions of our financial income and gain with God, He will be faithful to bless us. The Lord will bless those who bless Him, He longs for a people who will trust Him and bring a tithe offering.

"My son, do not reject the discipline of the LORD or loathe His reproof, for whom the LORD loves He reproves, even as a father corrects the son in whom he delights."

Proverbs 3:11-12

4. Proverbs 3:11-12 talk about discipline. Why does God discipline His people?

5. Verses 13-18 specifically address wisdom, described here as a woman. What are the benefits and blessings that wisdom brings those who "hold her fast"?

Wisdom brings so many positive results to our lives such as: long life, riches, honor, peace, life, happiness, and of course, understanding. This passage describes wisdom as more precious than profit gained from fine metals like silver and gold. Godly wisdom cannot be traded in a consumer market, or worn like a necklace; it has to be experienced through a connection to the source of true understanding; Jesus Christ.

A Closer Look:

If we fully believe that life isn't about us, then why would we strive to find our purpose outside of God's guidance? By putting our own desires and goals aside, we allow the Lord to reign in our lives in ways we never could have imagined. The commands of God and the Word of the Lord become our mission statement. God's truth defines our purpose. God's message fuels our calling. God calls the shots; not our imaginations, dreams, or best attempt at defining our own purpose by using our own wisdom.

As the Lord leads our heart, and our lives incorporate a constant reliance on the Word of God, our actions will reflect our beliefs in increasing measure. We will tithe and become more generous to the ministries around us. We will welcome God's correction when we stray. And, by not leaning on our own understanding while relying on God, we will enjoy the benefits of living according to His wisdom.

A Question for Your Life Today:

In Proverbs 3:7 there is a warning against being "wise in your own eyes." Has there been a time when you relied on your own wisdom over God's wisdom, and things didn't work out so well? Write out how it went wrong, and how you think God's wisdom could have helped the situation:

DAY FOUR

KEEPING ON OUR TOES – PROVERBS 3:19-26

The Focus Verse:

For the LORD will be your confidence and will keep your foot from being caught.
Proverbs 3:26

The Main Thought:

God's wisdom is best.

The Story within the Story:

Okay, so I'm a chicken—a full-fledged, non-athletic chicken. You won't find me on a ski slope peering over the summit at the run below with two toothpicks strapped to my boots. You won't catch me rock climbing with nothing but a rope keeping me from careening to my death. You certainly won't ever see me jumping out of a perfectly good airplane with all my trust wrapped up in a little piece of fabric hidden in a backpack strapped to my back. Terra firma; that's my goal—two feet planted firmly on ground that doesn't shake, rattle, or roll.

During a mission trip to Brazil, I had the opportunity to come face to face with my fear of heights. Being the only shivering scaredy cat in a group of travelers, I kept silent about my hesitation to ride the cable car to the top of a famous mountain. *Oh, the view would be spectacular, but is there any other way to get there?* I thought to myself. Looking straight up at Sugar Loaf Mountain in Rio, I had a talk with God about trust. Do I trust Him? Yes. Even riding in a little box up a rope to the top of a mountain? I guess. Like I said, I am a complete chicken.

As the rest of my team stood by the front window of the cable car and had a great time peering over the railing looking at the depths below, I was planted in the middle of the car, grabbing the railing with all my might and squeezing my eyes shut as tightly as I could manage. Not what I would consider fun. Did I mention it takes two cars to get there? Up to one mountaintop station, then get out and board more little cars to reach the higher peak.

Somehow, by the time we reached that second dock, my fear was gone. The Lord had truly given me a peace that only He could give. Chicken girl was now a semi-brave woman. I knew that my life was in God's hands and the only way I would survive the ordeal was to totally trust in Him. No matter the outcome, I knew that God was with me…on the mountaintop or stuck in a loose cable car plunging toward the water.

Maybe that's why I like today's passage so much. The Lord provides safe travels. He is there with us, even in danger. The Word provides a firm place to stand, giving us stability in our lives that keep us from stumbling. God promises that we can live without fear when we rely on Him. My Father in heaven is my "terra firma." Amen!

- Contentment.
- Safety.
- God's love.

That's what I read in the seven verses for today. Praise God for His comforting Word—especially for chickens like me.

The Passage:

Read Proverbs 3:19-26. Write down key points from the text and journal your thoughts about what you have read:

The Details:

1. Look at Proverbs 3:19-20. What do these two verses describe? What do they confirm from other passages we've studied?

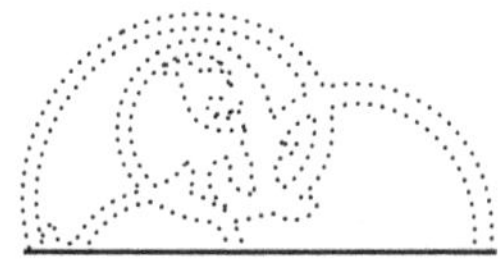

By His wisdom, the Lord created the heavens and the earth.

Today's passage re-confirms the truths of creation from the first chapter of our study. God is the Creator of earth, the heavens, and the rain that falls. God knew the Flood was coming in Noah's time, and caused the water to burst forth (Genesis 7:11). Even in that season of destruction, God called Noah to build the ark, in a plan to preserve His people and the animals. Through Noah's obedience to God's wisdom, the ark and all who were safely inside survived the Flood, and continued to thrive once back on land.

2. According to Proverbs 3:21-22, what two things are we to keep or preserve? Why?

3. Sound wisdom and discretion (NASB description) will be "life to your soul" (v. 22). Having such wisdom gives the benefits described in verses 23-26. List the benefits below:

We will walk and not stumble, sleep sweetly, and live free of the fear of disaster. Why? "The Lord will be your confidence, and will keep your foot from being caught" (v. 26).

A Closer Look:

Here are some key points we have learned together:

- God created.
- He established.
- His wisdom prevails.
- God has our best in mind.
- Believers are blessed when they walk in the wisdom of the Lord.
- God's wisdom keeps us from stumbling.

Throughout today's study, we have seen the affirmation of these points, and the comfort of knowing we are safe in the arms of the Lord. We don't have to fear, knowing that our hope is in the Lord. Isn't that the most exciting thing? Even in the "worst case scenario" of life, God is there. He understands, He loves us, and has great things in store for those who follow Him. We can trust that He has our best in mind.

A Question for Your Life Today:

According to Proverbs 3:14, what is the value of wisdom and understanding?

DAY FIVE

Walking Closely – Proverbs 3:27-35

The Focus Verse:

For the devious are an abomination to the Lord; but He is intimate with the upright.
Proverbs 3:32

The Main Thought:

Don't hold back!

The Story within the Story:

A man works for his wages. A job is agreed to with salary in mind and an expectation of payment for services rendered. Easy enough scenario, but what if the employer doesn't pay up? What happens to the person who puts in all those hours serving his boss? He experiences a major loss of time, energy, and potential payment from another job. In an ideal world, this type of fraud would never occur. In our reality, it happens every day.

One fellow I know worked his whole life for a major manufacturing company. Six months before the guy was planning to retire, in a completely unexpected move, the business filed for bankruptcy. This faithful worker lost his pension; his future provision. After 30-something years, the pension account he had faithfully paid into was suddenly gone. *Gone.* His entire retirement nest egg went up in smoke in the blink of an eye. Retirement never came.

Another worker got a job with a fast-paced business in a high-class metropolitan area. Work for a commission; that's the plan. He made sales, completed his work, and filed his paperwork, but there was no check. No money. No payment. This happened month after month. The dedicated salesman continued to press ahead, closing deals, and waiting for compensation. The money never came. Having enough of the false promises and fraudulent withholding of commissions earned, the worker hung his head, picked up his file box, and left the job with payment still due.

In both of these cases, the men who were taken advantage of found strength in the Lord. No matter what the employers did, God provided for the needs of the men and their families. By trusting in the Lord and persevering through the toughest of times, God was glorified. Soon they acquired new jobs, put paychecks into bank accounts, and put dinner back on the table. What about the anger and disappointment, you ask? Well, times were tough, but these men understood that God will fight our battles. In both cases, God revealed the wickedness of the crooked men who withheld what rightfully belonged to the employees. God brought justice.

The Passage:

Read Proverbs 3:27-35. Write down key points from the text and journal your thoughts about what you have read:

____

____

The Details:

1. What admonishment is given in verse 27?

____

____

____

2. After reading verse 28, picture the scene of the verse. How would you react if you asked your neighbor for help, and even though they had what you needed, they told you to come back another day?

____

____

3. What so verses 29-31 tell us?

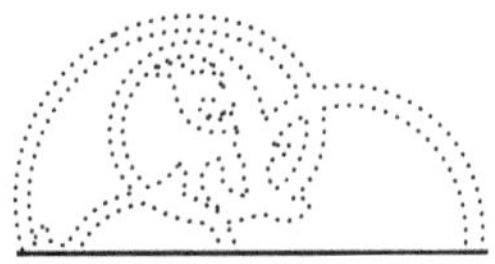

"For the devious are an abomination to the LORD; but He is intimate with the upright."

Proverbs 3:32

These verses sound a lot like the Ten Commandments, don't they? Love God, love others. Don't hurt people, pick a fight, or envy others. If we love others, we won't have those sorts of problems arise.

4. Proverbs 3:32-35 sum up our chapter, and tell us the bottom line of trusting in the Lord. Describe the passage:

As we see in verse 32, believers of God Most High are not an abomination; we are keepers of His "secret" (KJV) or "intimate" with God (NASB). Both of these words are translated from the Hebrew word *sod*, which refers to God establishing "a close, intimate relationship with those who revere Him and walk uprightly" (*The Complete Word Study Dictionary: Old Testament,* p. 771). Far from something disgraceful, we become keepers of a special friendship, partakers of a sweet fellowship with God. How wonderful it is to be loved by our Savior.

A Closer Look:

Much like our Ten Commandments study session, the principles found in Proverbs 3 lead us closer to the feet of Jesus and more in line with the will of the Father. By leaning on the wisdom of God and trusting Him with all our heart, we gain blessing, understanding, and fellowship with the Creator. We are brought closer in our relationship with the Lord and we are admonished when we stray. We are protected from those who mean us harm and we are expected not to harm others. Loving God and loving others is the focus once again, our theme for Christian living.

A Question for Your Life Today:

In this lesson, we discovered that if we keep God's commands and walk in His ways, it will be easier to seek Him and lean on Him for understanding and answers to life's problems. In light of this, how will you change daily habits and schedules in order to follow God more intensely?

____

____

____

____

____

WORKS CITED:

Baker, Warren and Eugene Carpenter, eds. *The Complete Word Study Dictionary: Old Testament.* Chattanooga: AMG Publishers, 2003:

Hesed, #2617, p. 360.

Sekel, #7922, p. 1138.

Biynah, #998, p. 130.

Hakam, #2450, p. 336.

Sod, #5475, p. 770-771.

WEEK FOUR

God of All Comfort

The Valley

Psalm 23

This famous psalm always reminds me of funerals. It speaks of a need for comfort in the midst of despair—a common passage to mark the season of leaving this world. Walking "through the valley of the shadow of death" (Psalm 23:4) has taken a slightly different meaning than David's original intention as he fled the danger of persecution at the hand of King Saul. Most of those who are remembered with such a passage haven't gone through the continuous strife that David had endured. Nonetheless, the truth hidden in the words are comfort to any who are experiencing loss and grief. The verses give us the eternal hope that God is with us, even in the midst of pain.

When my earthly father passed away, we faced many decisions. As we made the funeral preparations, one of the easiest things to decide was the memorial card Scripture passage. We chose Psalm 23. It looked wonderful on the back of the flyer and was a very present reminder of the Lord who watched over us that day. Through our tears, we were blessed by reading these words of encouragement. Our pastor also used this psalm in his message, speaking the words of hope we so desperately needed to hear.

The timeless words of faith first spoken centuries ago by David are healing words to the soul. They comfort even the most broken-hearted. The words of the psalm point to a hope beyond what is seen—to the hope of eternity. The day we buried my father, no other words could have captured the love of our Shepherd. No one but God the Father could have brought such peace as we struggled through one of the most difficult and emotionally painful days of our lives.

Psalm 23 has become a familiar passage between believers and unbelievers alike. Why? It seems that in our culture this familiar sound byte appeals to many, whether they relate to the quote in context or not. All too often we quote soothing words without stopping to think about what the psalmist was going through, or what trials he faced, while writing the words. This week we will see how David, the man after God's own heart, fought for his life against Saul, the jealous ruler. Over and over, David escaped the perilous traps that Saul set. God, the source of all comfort, carried David through this season, and eventually rewarded the young shepherd with King Saul's position and throne.

Pain, loss, and agony seem to be the precursors to using this psalm for times of reflection. Life application tends to be limited to comfort for the bereaved, the sick, the hurting, the lost, and the down and out. Let us not forget that there is also an underlying sense of victory, provision, and blessing in the verses of the Twenty-Third Psalm. It is a record of victory over enemies, comfort in the midst of trial, and acknowledgement of God's tremendous blessings. An unlikely victory song, this passage gives all of us hope in the depths of helplessness, love in the agony of pain, and confidence in the midst of persecution. God's love shines forth from the valley to the pastures, the quiet running streams, and the banquet table of blessing.

DAY ONE

The Great Shepherd – Psalm 23:1

The Focus Verse:

The LORD is my shepherd, I shall not want. **Psalm 23:1**

The Main Thought:

The Lord is our source of contentment.

The Story within the Story:

Young David would have understood the role of a shepherd. As a boy, he wandered the meadows with sheep in tow, working long hours keeping the flocks. As the boy grew, so did the calling on his life. I imagine an older David writing this psalm and daydreaming of times when life was easy. After all, it was a much simpler life back then. Pick up your staff, round up the sheep, and head for a pleasant meadow. Look after the helpless animals and keep them safe. Only through trial and tribulation did it become evident that the Lord had trained David in essential leadership skills and traits during his time as a shepherd. God taught the young boy how to care for others, protect the needy, and continually be on watch against predators.

David, the man after God's own heart, was a caregiver to the wooly little creatures until Saul called him to serve in the kingdom. David had his infamous run-in with the giant after coming straight from the sheepfold to the battlefield to visit his brothers. No sophisticated armor or weapons would do for this rural warrior; smooth stones and a sling shot were the weapon of choice for this young shepherd. The skill for aiming little rocks was no doubt gained while protecting the sheep in the pasture from sneaky predators.

As a former shepherd, David truly understood what it meant to provide such intimate leadership. At the time this psalm was being written, I imagine David must have felt quite helpless; running from Saul and feeling as though there was no defense stronger than the help of a shepherd. David understood that God was His shepherd, and that the Lord would have to fight his battles for him. The persecuted leader sought contentment in the Lord, not wanting for anything but what He could provide.

The Passage:

Read Psalm 23:1. Write down key points from the text and journal your thoughts about what you have read:

The Details:

1. How does David describe the Lord in Psalm 23:1?

____

____

____

The term "shepherd" was commonly used in that time to refer to a king. David, a young shepherd, certainly acknowledged the Lord as King of his life, and understood the relationship of a shepherd and his sheep. It should come as no surprise that David would make reference to a shepherd in his writings, since that role was so integral to his own life story. David spent his youth watching over the family flock until the Lord brought him as a servant to Saul's kingdom. Let's look into David's background and his history with Saul.

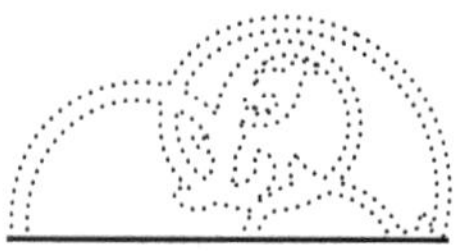

"...and the Spirit of the LORD came mightily upon David from that day forward..."

1 Samuel 16:13

2. Look up 1 Samuel 16:11-13. What is described in this passage?

____

____

____

Leading up to this scene, the Lord was displeased with the sins of Saul, and called His prophet Samuel to go and anoint the next king. God told Samuel that one of the sons of Jesse the Bethlehemite would be the one chosen. When Samuel arrived at Jesse's house and met his children, he knew that God had not chosen any of the sons presented. Asking for any other children, Samuel discovered David out in the pasture, tending sheep. Samuel anointed David and the Holy Spirit came upon David, giving him favor with God and man.

3. Read 1 Samuel 16:14-18. How did David wind up meeting Saul for the first time? What was Saul looking for?

____

____

____

In verse 18, what qualities were used to describe David?

4. According to 1 Samuel 16:19, where was David when they sent for him?

David, the boy of many talents, became the minstrel for King Saul, playing soothing music to keep an evil spirit away. The servant had described the young man as a mighty warrior, valiant, a good musician, handsome, and so forth: overstating his qualities and qualifications in order to please the king. While he may not have possessed such qualities as a child, David became many of these things in later years!

5. 1 Samuel 16:20-23 describes the relationship David had with Saul early in his life. What was David's job, and what was the result of his work?

6. 1 Samuel 17:15 sheds more light on David's experience as a shepherd. What does this verse reveal?

David was clearly dedicated to his father and the family flock. He played the harp for the king, and served as a shepherd at home. We see his humility and dedication portrayed over and over throughout his life.

7. Read 1 Samuel 17:55-58, and then 1 Samuel 18:3.What happened in this next exchange between Saul and David? Did Saul act as if he remembered David?

____

____

____

While David engaged in minstrel service, his brothers had gone off to fight the Philistines. When Jesse asked his youngest son to take supplies to the brothers, the famous scene with David and Goliath took place. David was victorious against Goliath, and, as a result, Saul kept the victorious stone-thrower close to himself. Through this background information, we see how the relationship between the two men was established.

David understood the relationship between a shepherd and his sheep. He had spent many hours protecting, caring for, and leading the flock in his care. The young shepherd understood the role of caretaker and the necessity for such leadership. Sheep are totally lost without a shepherd. They do not know where to go or what to do without someone leading them on the right path.

Why would David refer to God as his shepherd?

____

____

____

8. Read John 10:1-18. Who is the shepherd in this passage? What is His role? (v.11)

____

____

____

9. Now read the second half of Psalm 23:1. Write what it says:

"*I shall not want.*" What significance do you think this has, coupled with the first part of the verse's association of God as a shepherd? What do you think David's statement means?

"I am the good shepherd; the good shepherd lays down His life for the sheep."

John 10:11

In this simple verse, David acknowledges his dependence on God, and his trust in the Lord to bring all provision.

10. Compare this with Psalm 34:9-10. What additional information does David share about "not wanting"? Describe the verses, and the association with being godly and finding contentment.

What areas of your life do you struggle with the issue of being content? Describe ways that you can lean more fully on the Lord for your sense of peace and fulfillment:

Write down some awesome ways that God has already provided for you and your family and blessed your life. Take a moment to praise Him for these blessings:

A Closer Look:

Using a reference from his own life experience, David refers to the Father as his shepherd, or the leader of his life. Speaking through submission and dependence on God, the young shepherd begins this psalm in affirmation of the Lordship of God over those who follow Him.

As a man who acknowledges that the Lord is His shepherd, David understands that His God will provide all his needs. If our sufficiency is truly in God, we will not seek earthly treasure and gain--we will find contentment in the Lord. David recognizes that our sufficiency, our provision, and our peace are found in the Lord. With our trust in God, we will not "want" for anything.

In John 10:1-18, Jesus shares a parable about a shepherd and his sheep. Jesus explains His role in this parable in verse 11 saying, "I am the good shepherd; the good shepherd lays down His life for the sheep." The greatest gift a shepherd has for his flock is protection; the greatest gift Jesus could give was Himself. As our great shepherd, Jesus has provided the ultimate sacrifice and in doing so He protects all who are His from eternal separation from God and eternity in hell.

A Question for Your Life Today:

Imagine God as our Shepherd, and us as His sheep. If our "world" is our pasture, and we roam within the boundaries set by the Shepherd, shouldn't we feel safe? Along that same thought if the Shepherd's boundaries are the same as God's will for our lives, describe how we are safe if we seek to stay in God's will for our lives:

DAY TWO

Times of Refreshing – Psalm 23:2-3

The Focus Verse:

He restores my soul; He guides me in the paths of righteousness. Psalm 23:3

The Main Thought:

God gives us peace.

The Story within the Story:

Calgon®, take me away! Remember those commercials? In a 30-second sales pitch for bubble bath, the commercial's story line portrayed a woman at her wits end who locks herself in the bathroom and takes a bubble bath to relax. Calgon®, the bubbly stuff, apparently made her forget all her stress and gave the poor woman a needed boost.

As a kid, I thought that commercial was the silliest thing I ever saw; after all, who would ever get so stressed that they would want a bubble bath in the middle of the day? Why would moms need a break? I used to giggle at the television ad because it seemed so unrealistic. Oh the follies of youth.

As an adult, I understand that TV commercial more than I'd like to admit. When the day is busy and life is coming at me full speed, I think of that woman in her bathtub and smile. I finally relate to her plight. Some days, I long to sneak upstairs, put my pajamas on, and curl up with a cup of coffee and a good book. Unfortunately, that just never seems to work out. *Maybe if I had some Calgon®. . .*

The love of God restores our soul so much more than a bubble bath or favorite novel ever could. We will find whispers of rest and relaxation, times of refreshing, and glimpses of sweet fellowship—if we seek the Lord and meet with Him in the quiet moments of our day. Today's verses will show us the gentle love of our Savior, and the way He woos us into paths of righteousness. May we take time to find God in the pastures of our days and by the waterside of life.

The Passage:

Read Psalm 23:2-3. Write down key points from the text and journal your thoughts about what you have read:

The Details:

1. Read Psalm 23:2. What does this verse describe?

In light of Psalm 23:1, what reference would this have to a shepherd's sheep? Why would a green pasture and quiet waters be a benefit?

Can you just picture it? The Lord leads us to green pastures and cool waters of rest. Little sheep in need of a safe haven are protected from harm by their master. Oh, how we need this today, just as desperately as David did. Let's look and see how the young shepherd went from Saul's minstrel to the king's enemy.

2. What happens in 1 Samuel 18:10-16?

3. Read 1 Samuel 19:1-12. What is the relationship between Saul and David at this point?

Who protects David in these verses?

Saul turns on David, and begins to come up with ways to hurt or kill David. Even the king's own son, Jonathan, and daughter, Michal, protect the young man. Over and over through the book of 1 Samuel we read of Saul's dislike for David's prosperity and success and the many attempts on David's life. David, a man of mercy and integrity, has many opportunities to kill Saul, but refrains. David, the man after God's own heart, chooses to let God bring the victory.

It is with this relationship between king and servant that we find such admiration for the psalmist's words. Even while hiding out in caves and safe havens, David praises the Lord. No matter what chaos encircles him, David praises God for His protection, and acknowledges that it is the Lord who leads him to peace.

4. Read Psalm 23:3. What impact does God have on our soul?

Where does God guide us?

What for?

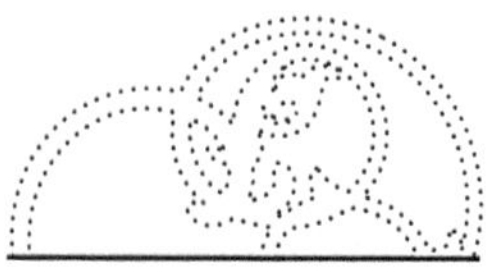

"Righteousness," or *sedeq* in Hebrew, refers to a straight path – one narrowly following the will of the Father. A person who walks in righteousness will not stray from the Lord's commands.

God is not only our peace, He restores us. He guides us to His will. The Lord leads us to Himself; to paths of righteousness. Through our walk with the Savior, we have rest, restoration, and righteousness. No matter what we face, or who may be chasing us. Now that's a promise!

A Closer Look:

In order to cultivate our relationship with the Lord, we must be willing to spend time in fellowship with our Savior. By spending time in prayer, reading the Word of God, study, and fellowship with other believers, we learn more about God. We grow in our relationship with Him. The more we understand God and converse with Him through prayer, the more we will learn to follow His lead and obey His voice. Through a lifetime of spiritual growth, we will learn how to take moments of rest in the pastures the Lord provides and drink from the cool waters offered us. God will sustain us, but we have to be available and willing to listen.

A Question for Your Life Today:

Think of a stressful time in your life; past or present. Now read Psalm 23:3. What is the type of comfort described in this verse? How would that comfort impact the stresses of our lives?

DAY THREE

No Fear – Psalm 23:4

The Focus Verse:

Even though I walk through the valley of the shadow of death, I fear no evil, for You are with me; Your rod and Your staff, they comfort me. **Psalm 23:4**

The Main Thought:

No fear with God.

The Story within the Story:

Every generation has "that day" in their memory. For the World War 2 generation it was Pearl Harbor and D-Day. In the Kennedy era, it was the assassinations. Today, unfortunately, we have 9/11. Almost every American could tell you where they were, what they were doing, and how they were affected by the tragedies of those horrific days in our nation's history. We remember. We should remember. But, as we remember, let's think about the source of our comfort. God is the God who comforts us in our darkest hours; even in the "valley of the shadow of death."

Living through traumatic events, illness, and even death of a loved one can seem to steal every inkling of peace from our lives. As for our family, we were personally affected by 9/11, but blessed in spite of the events of the day. Rather than tell you the earthly details, I want to share with you a major spiritual lesson from that tragedy. In the midst of crisis, I didn't stop to allow God to fully comfort me. I prayed for safety and thought I was leaning on the Lord, but my fear and reactions in those moments revealed to me my lack of complete dependence on the God of all comfort.

Instead of the peace of the Lord ruling my thoughts, the fear of the potential loss of my spouse drove my seconds, minutes, and hours. Around three in the afternoon, when I finally found out he was alive, I was able to take a deep breath and praise the Lord. Oh, how I wish I had let the Lord be my *complete* comfort between ten and three. Even as a believer, I have so much room for growth. In the midst of our storm, we were blessed with a report of life and safety. I grieve for the families who are unable to say the same, and pray that God will be a powerful part of their lives.

I learned a tough lesson in that urgent situation; don't let panic and fear take the place of the comfort of God. I praise God every day that my husband is alive and by my side. I also praise God that He has taught me more about finding comfort in the midst of crisis, and understanding our victory in Jesus.

The Passage:

Read Psalm 23:4. Write down key points from the text and journal your thoughts about what you have read:

____

____

____

The Details:

1. What does the first half of Psalm 23:4 talk about? What is David facing while writing this psalm?

____

____

____

The "valley of the shadow of death" is also referred to as the "valley of deep darkness." *The Complete Word Study Dictionary: Old Testament,* (p. 953) describes the Hebrew word *salmawet* as a "death shadow, a deep shadow." It is interesting to note that this phrase mentions the "shadow" of death – not death itself, but the shadow of it; the imminent, looming, or danger of death. This term has also been used to relate to death, darkened understanding, or spiritual darkness.

David was under constant attack and persecution from Saul. No matter how merciful he tried to be or how upright his honor, David remained in danger. Saul wanted David dead. Even in such darkness and despair, the young shepherd learned to find his comfort in the Lord.

Read the second half of Psalm 23:4 and write out the source of David's comfort:

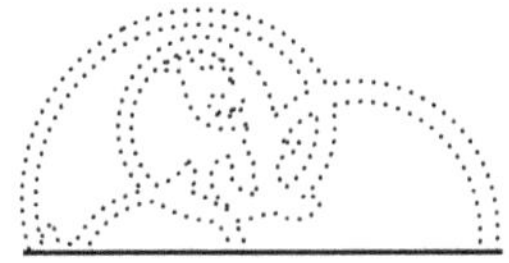

"Comfort," or *naham* in Hebrew, refers to God's consoling love, compassion, and care for His children who are hurting. God's comfort for David was birthed out of His compassion for the follower.

A Closer Look:

David found comfort in his ever-present faith that God was with him. He also mentions God's rod and staff in this verse. Just as a shepherd guides his flock with the staff he carries, the Lord guides His followers with a rod and staff. The rod was a symbol of authority and was used to number the sheep. Jesus knows us by name and knows those who are His. Through His love for us, the Lord keeps us on track and on the narrow path.

Whether we are fearful of death, looking into the face of death, or grieving the death of a loved one, God is our shepherd. As Jesus taught, if we are under His care, we know His voice. We are protected by His commands. And we are comforted by His love. David understood the magnitude of Saul's threats, but even then, he acknowledged God's position as the ultimate authority and loving caretaker of his life.

A Question for Your Life Today:

No matter what we go through in our lives, the last line of Psalm 23 gives us a sweet promise: "surely goodness and lovingkindness will follow me all the days of my life, and I will dwell in the house of the Lord forever" (Psalm23:6). In light of the beginning of the Psalm, where we learned about God being with us in difficult times, how does this verse encourage us when bad things happen?

DAY FOUR

God's Abundant Blessings – Psalm 23:5

The Focus Verse:

You prepare a table before me in the presence of my enemies; You have anointed my head with oil; my cup overflows. Psalm 23:5

The Main Thought:

God blesses us, even when man comes against us.

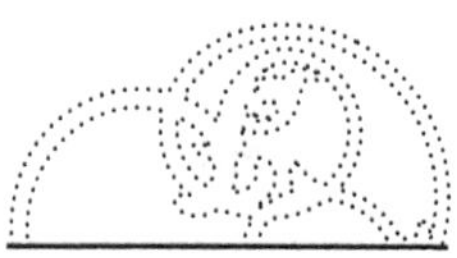

"David said to Saul, 'Why do you listen to the words of men, saying, "Behold, David seeks to harm you?" Behold, this day your eyes have seen that the LORD had given you today into my hand in the cave, and some said to kill you, but *my* eye had pity on you; and I said, "I will not stretch out my hand against my lord, for he is the LORD's anointed."'

1 Samuel 24:9-10

The Story within the Story:

Not just peace in days of trouble, but joy in the midst of danger, today's verse contains words that make reference to God's presence in days of persecution. Who would assert such things? David, the man after God's own heart would. He was the boy who spent most of his days on the run.

After initial death threats and the protection of Michal and Jonathan, David continued to seek refuge from the schemes of an angry Saul. Many times, David had opportunity to retaliate, yet he refrained. The young anointed shepherd showed mercy toward the persecutor, as shown in passages like 1 Samuel 24, where we have proof that David spared Saul's life.

In this recorded tale, David sneaks up on Saul while the leader takes a break in a dark cave. David definitely had the upper hand, and the pleasure of deciding the fate of the surprised leader. Would it be death for a king? No. Only a corner of Saul's robe was cut; a secret act revealing the merciful heart of the persecuted man.

David felt remorse even for this action and quickly went out and talked with Saul. In humility and reverence, while refraining from harming the angry king, David asked simple questions and longed for his pure motives to be known. He tried to convince the king that he was safe from the servant's sword.

You would think that Saul would show mercy toward David because of his loyalty. At least you would think. Somehow, Saul was never satisfied with such petitions. The king continued to issue death threats toward David and yet through it all, David continued to rely on the Lord.

Through a variety of life experiences, David poured out his heart to the Lord in his psalms. Our verse for today speaks of finding contentment, blessing, and God's equipping power, all learned by David as he fled from the hands of Saul.

The Passage:

Read Psalm 23:5. Write down key points from the text and journal your thoughts about what you have read:

____

____

____

The Details:

1. Psalm 23:5 proclaims that God provides even in the midst of turmoil. How does David word this truth?

____

____

____

A table is prepared when provision is at hand. We set the dinner table before we sit down for an evening meal, and in the same way, the Lord sets His will and direction before us as we follow His lead. But look! God doesn't just prepare the table; He also does so "in the presence of David's enemies." God is not fearful of man and his evil schemes. The Lord reigns over all things and is able to bless His followers in the most unusual circumstances. As Saul sought David's demise, God provided blessing.

2. Write out the second portion of today's verse.

Anointing with oil is God's way of ceremonially equipping those He calls to service. It is a sign of God's blessing coming upon the person. Remember when Samuel chose David?

3. Look again at 1 Samuel 16:12-13. Who deemed David worthy of anointing? How did Samuel then anoint him, and how did God equip David as a result of the anointing?

Samuel heard the Lord say that David was the person He was calling. Then Samuel anointed David with oil he carried in a horn, and God equipped David by sending His Holy Spirit upon him. David understood that the anointing was a sign of God's blessing.

4. Look at Psalm 133, another famous psalm of David's that talks about Christian unity. How does he relate unity to the blessing of being anointed? Describe the passage:

Unity among believers is described as anointing oil flowing down Aaron's head and robes, signifying the people of God receiving abundant blessing from God as they joined together in service to their King.

A Closer Look:

Anointing oil is used to consecrate God's people for service or to bring forth God's blessing. When something or someone is anointed, they are strengthened or filled. In this passage of Psalm 23, the anointing oil signified a joy that the Lord brought to David, even on the run and when hiding out. David finishes Psalm 23:5 with a powerful statement: "my cup overflows." Contentment. Satisfaction. Sufficiency. Blessing. God is there . . . *in the midst.*

Take a moment to praise God for giving you an overflowing cup—for the times when the Lord has been there for you, even in the midst of hard times.

A Question for Your Life Today:

If the Shepherd's boundaries are the same as God's will for our lives, describe how we are safe if we seek to stay in God's will for our lives.

____

____

____

DAY FIVE

Eternal God – Psalm 23:6

The Focus Verse:

Surely goodness and lovingkindness will follow me all the days of my life, and I will dwell in the house of the LORD *forever.* **Psalm 23:6**

The Main Thought:

Eternal life awaits those who believe in God.

The Story within the Story:

No matter our lot, the Lord is with us. The promise of salvation awaits those who trust in Him. Eternity beckons. In the most frustrating, painful moments of life, do we remember this promise? Do we celebrate the hereafter, here and now? Does this realization get shuffled to the bottom of the pile of our thoughts? Oh, that we would live as if we have such a promise! Imagine if every day we rose from slumber in praise to our God for His unmerited favor toward His children. Think about the impact believers could have on the world around them if we all planned our days and lived our lives sharing, believing, and remembering that we already walk in victory over the grave through Jesus Christ.

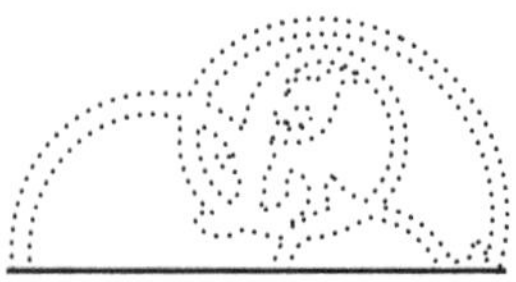

Trust in God's love and goodness while you're living, and live in light of the hope of eternity.

David is such an inspiration to us all as he traveled through the years hiding from the enemy, standing up to evil, and reigning in victory. No matter the struggle, David stood as a man of faith, willing to face every obstacle with the Lord by his side. David knew the source of his victory!

In this last verse of the Twenty-Third Psalm, David reveals an essential secret to all God followers: trust in God's love and goodness while you're living, and live in light of the hope of eternity. When this life is over, our relationship with the Lord will not end; it will continue forever. What a promise! By focusing on this timeless truth, we will tap into God's joy—in the midst of pain, trial and persecution.

The Passage:

Read Psalm 23:6. Write down key points from the text and journal your thoughts about what you have read:

The Details:

1. According to the first part of Psalm 23:6, what two things follow David all of his life?

____

____

____

2. Where will David, and all believers, dwell forever?

____

____

____

Goodness and lovingkindness are with him and eternity with the Lord is assured. What confidence this psalmist has in his relationship with his Lord. Remember when we studied *lovingkindness*? This powerful term for the overwhelming love of God is used here to reaffirm that God's mercy, love, and kindness are with us in our darkest trials. Coupled with the praise of a worshiper, and the faith that goodness and lovingkindness are possible, David confirms his faith with the address of his final home.

A Closer Look:

Let's look at truths tucked into this week's passage:

- God is in control.
- God provides all we need.
- God gives us peace.
- God refreshes our soul.
- God keeps us on the right path.
- God's presence casts out fear.
- God's direction provides comfort.

- God blesses us, even while enduring persecution
- God equips us and strengthens us
- God brings joy in life
- God promises eternity for His followers

Notice a major theme? Yep. *It's all about God.* Our six verses from Psalm 23 speak of a mighty God with a loving heart. They remind us of the many ways that the Lord's presence is felt by those who trust in Him. No matter the shadows in the valley, our God will prevail, and cause us to triumph.

A Question for Your Life Today:

What encouragement do you find in this truth, knowing that no matter what happens in your lifetime, as a believer you will be with the Lord forever?

____

____

____

____

____

WORKS CITED:

Baker, Warren and Eugene Carpenter, eds. *The Complete Word Study Dictionary: Old Testament.* Chattanooga: AMG Publishers, 2003:

Salmawet, #6757, p. 953.

Sedeq, #6664, p. 938.

Naham, #5162, p. 723.

WEEK FIVE

Eternal God

God's Timing

Ecclesiastes 3:1-14

I'll never forget my first day in Panama. Before we traveled to our new home, my husband continually affirmed that we were going to a tropical paradise. "It'll be great! We'll love it there!" he'd say. Yet the first glimpses of paradise weren't anything like he had described. Peeking out the airplane window, I couldn't find much of a paradise at all. The first thing I noticed about Panama was the brush fires. We arrived in the middle of the dry season, and when the heat is mixed with the dry weather, the rainforest tends to spontaneously erupt with little bonfires. From the air, it seemed pretty scary, and as I looked out the window, I found it hard to view the tropical paradise through the smoke rising from the patches of fire. Little did I know it was just part of the dry season.

The season did eventually change, but not by much. Panama only has two seasons: wet and dry. No big temperature changes, no colorful falling leaves, and definitely no snow. For months on end we would have rain in an increasing measure, followed by a few months of no rain at all. Lush rainforest flora bloomed and filled the landscape with more varieties of green foliage than I had ever seen before. Beautiful flowers and interesting fruit hung from branches, drawing little creatures out of the safety of the jungle's cover to their branch buffets. From brushfires to monsoon rains, our family became acclimated to our new country and the shifting from drought to flood. We did eventually love it there, but it took awhile for the jungle to grow on us.

The only one who had major problems with the months of rain was my pug Sasha. She was a true puppy princess who didn't like to get her paws wet. Imagine, walking a dog for months on end in monsoon season, while trying not to get wet. It was comical, really. Armed with an oversized umbrella, she and I would head out the back door, aiming straight for the dry ground under the palm tree. As soon as she was safely under the fronds of that tree and sheltered from the downpour, she'd quickly take care of business and tip toe back to the house. Seriously; she tip toed. Anything to keep the princess's paws as dry as possible. If the rain was really beating down, she'd dig her front feet in and rear back like a donkey, stubbornly refusing to go outside. It is safe to say that she didn't do well with the seasons of Panama.

The seasons of life come and go, sometimes with more drama than brushfires and monsoons. We rejoice and grieve, celebrate and mourn, laugh and cry. Each day brings its own challenges and triumphs. But as we learned last week, no matter what life throws our way, we can live with a confidence that God is in control. He is our comfort, our help in danger, and our joy in daily life.

DAY ONE

A Life or Death Proposition – Ecclesiastes 3:1-3

The Focus Verse:

There is an appointed time for everything. And there is a time for every event under heaven. **Ecclesiastes 3:1**

The Main Thought:

Seasons come and go, just as life begins and ends.

The Story within the Story:

The process of getting flowerbeds ready for spring begins long before the weather gets warm. In fact, spring planting begins in the fall. Before the frost hits the ground, the spring bulbs are tenderly placed at the right depth in the soil and prepared for their joyous arrival. All winter long, the cold, rain, wind, and even snow pass over the surface of the beds, bringing the shock of harsh conditions. Yet, along with this colder weather come all the elements needed to force the flowers out of their bulbs. The bulbs get a taste of cold air, water, darkness, and time; all essential elements to spring growth.

In the long wait for spring to spring forth, it is easy to forget about the rows of bulbs waiting to sprout above the ground's surface. Since the bulbs went in long ago, it is easy to forget them until we see them coming up in the spring. The soil covers their presence, and eventually we cannot even remember where we planted them! The cold, harsh winters seem dreary and the bare tree limbs remind us more of death than new life. The scenery looks lifeless and cold. It feels as though spring will never come; just like our season of hibernation will seemingly never end.

Then one day it happens. Little bits of green leaves shoot through the hard dirt, and then they rise through the air, stretching their little shoots up toward heaven until each little flower begins to open. Spring just isn't spring without the crocus, tulips, and narcissus lining the flowerbeds of life. Oh, when the flowers are all in bloom, our whole outlook begins to change. *Spring is coming.* The winter season will cease to freeze, and new life will occur! In our darkest and coldest seasons of life, we must hold on to the hope that the Lord will bring forth a change. Our eternity with Him will come. Our joy will bloom again.

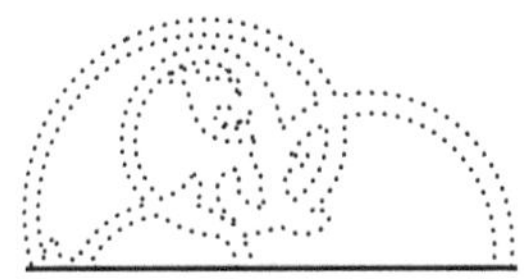

In our darkest and coldest seasons of life, we must hold on to the hope that the Lord will bring forth a change.

The Passage:

Read Ecclesiastes 3:1-3. Write down key points from the text and journal your thoughts about what you have read:

The Details:

1. What does Ecclesiastes 3:1 tell us?

___

___

___

The exact term for "appointed time" used here, *zeman* in Hebrew, is found only in Scripture three or four times. It is interesting to note that one of these other uses is found in Esther 9:27, where the Feast of Purim was to be scheduled and celebrated "according to their appointed time annually." The people of God established a feast of remembrance for an important time in their history—a remembrance to occur each year at the appointed time. This is definitely more of a regularly scheduled event than an unexpected arrival. Much like the annual biblical feasts, our yearly spring bloom is closely related to the appointed time of the thawing temperatures of spring.

2. Notice verse 2, and the combination of seasons listed. What is mentioned first?

___

___

___

Then what comparison is made?

___

___

___

I find it interesting that just as our Bible begins with creation, this listing of seasons in Ecclesiastes opens with the comparison of life and death. Truly, we are only here for a season—we are passing through. But look at the second part of verse two! Remember in the creation account how the first living creation was seed bearing plants? Here, we have life, then plants growing and being uprooted.

Why do you think Solomon began with life and death, planting, and uprooting?

3. Read Ecclesiastes 3:3. What contrasts do we read about in this verse?

How do these compare to verse two?

A Closer Look:

The first three verses of this week's passage give us an affirmation that life and death is a normal cycle. We all were born and we are all destined to pass from this world; either enjoying heaven or suffering in hell for eternity. Plant life also has the same cycle; it is planted and it grows, then it is uprooted. Such cycles of life are a given, and before we can talk about any other seasonal shift or appointed time, the Lord laid the foundation of seasons with life itself.

A Question for Your Life Today:

Years ago there was a bumper sticker that said, "The one who dies with the most toys wins." After reading this week's passage in Ecclesiastes, does it make sense to try and accumulate tons of stuff here on earth? Are we going to get to take a big truck full of possessions with us to heaven?

DAY TWO

Emotional Shift – Ecclesiastes 3:4-5

The Focus Verse:

A time to weep and a time to laugh; a time to mourn and a time to dance. Ecclesiastes 3:4

The Main Thought:

God turns our mourning into dancing.

The Story within the Story:

The 1960s flower child generation memorized these familiar verses while singing along with a popular tune. Did they realize as they played their favorite vinyl record on the turntable that the truths of God are so much more than manmade decisions driving the seasons of life? Did they relate more with the cynical desperation that Solomon felt as he wrote out his frustrations of life in the book of Ecclesiastes than the truths of the hope of salvation?

It is hard to look at this passage without humming the pop culture tune in our head. What is the lesson for us as believers? What do the words speak to us today? The words of Solomon speak of the futility of our own imaginations, experiences, and life cycle. Yet I see *hope*. I see eternity tucked between the lines. I see God all over this passage! Without His appointed times and seasons, our lives would lack the ups and downs that cause growth. We wouldn't have such a blessed opportunity to learn from our mistakes, to take the good with the bad, and to grow in times of struggle.

Most of our spiritual growth occurs while we are being shaped and molded through trial and perseverance. The seasons we face give us glimpses of what we are like "when the going gets tough," and what God has strengthened us to do. As we persevere, we learn how to allow God to take control of our lives and how to trust in His guidance and direction. We learn to let the Lord guide our seasons and to praise Him for the times when we reach victories and joy. We learn to praise God in the midst of joy and pain or happiness and sorrow.

The Passage:

Read Ecclesiastes 3:4-5. Write down key points from the text and journal your thoughts about what you have read:

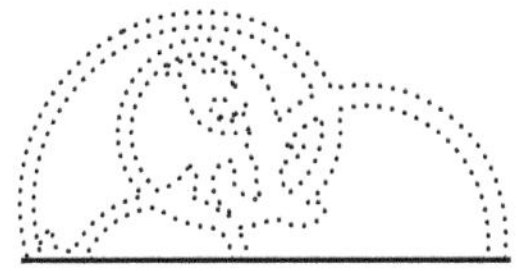

"Hope does not disappoint, because the love of God has been poured out within our hearts through the Holy Spirit who was given to us."

Romans 5:5

The Details:

1. Verse four describes some emotional ups and downs. Can you identify with the shift from weeping to laughing? Write about a time when an unexpectedly emotional season occurred:

What changed your weeping to laughing? What improved your outlook, bringing you from mourning to dancing?

Psalm 126:5 describes such a shift in emotion this way, "Those who sow in tears shall reap with joyful shouting." Each and every difficult experience or sad moment is like a seed planted for future use by the Lord. Seed time may grow into a beautiful display of the Lord's love. As Romans 8:28 reminds us, "We know that God causes all things to work together for good to those who love God, to those who are called according to *His* purpose." [*Emphasis added.*]

2. Read Ecclesiastes 3:5. What comparisons are made?

We can pursue many things while we live out our lives on this earth, but there is only one constant: no matter the season, no matter the stage of life, everything in between life and death falls short of our eternal destination. Our goal is eternity; we are just passing through.

A Closer Look:

Over the past two days we have seen appointed times, seasons, emotions, and actions come and go. We have thought about different times of our lives. What is the one constant in our lives? It is God and our relationship with Him. It hinges on our trust in the Lord to bring about good in every situation and to bring us into heaven to share eternity with Him.

While the favorite song of the flower child may have reminded them "to everything, turn, turn, turn . . ." and then quoted these verses in Ecclesiastes, the truth of God's presence in our lives goes far beyond our futility. God is with us in every season, in every appointed time, and in every trial. The power of God is seen when we realize that our life circumstances are truly things that occur "under heaven." One day we will be made new as we reign with the Lord in victory over the grave. A day is coming when there will be no more sadness, gloom, or despair for those who trust in the Lord.

A Question for Your Life Today:

Knowing that we are here for just a season, and we are able to serve God for a limited time in these earthly vessels we know as our bodies, how can we best serve God? Is being a busy person enough?

DAY THREE

Lost and Found – Ecclesiastes 3:6-7

The Focus Verse:

A time to search and a time to give up as lost; a time to keep and a time to throw away. **Ecclesiastes 3:6**

The Main Thought:

Everything comes and goes, but with the Lord, we never give up hope!

The Story within the Story:

Recently the news carried an amazing story of a found boy. Kidnapped years ago, and never forgotten, the child's posters were plastered all over the area. He never came home. Years dragged on and the abducted boy adapted to his new life as well as could be expected, although constant fear and a fake name kept him from his true identity and home. Even though years had gone by, his parents never gave up hope. They searched, they looked, they held on to the expectation that he would return to them. His room remained just as it was when he left. They knew he'd come home . . . someday.

Then one day while the police were searching for another missing child, they found two children! One was the newly-abducted child along with the boy from years ago. Two were found. Two returned home. Both acknowledged that they were held against their will and both chose to go back to their families. By no fault of their own, a thief had taken the children away and held them captive. But now freedom had brought them deliverance; brought them home again. For the children, life would never be like it was the day they left. For the older boy, life with his parents was something he had dreamed of for more than a decade. For the younger boy, it had only been days. In both cases, the reunion was sweet, and the homecomings were emotional. Thank God the parents never gave up their children. Thank God they did not simply dismiss them as "forever lost."

The Bible has a story about a child who was lost. It is our story. Without Jesus, "All have sinned and fall short of the glory of God" (Romans 3:23). Only through God's gift of redemption through Jesus Christ do we have the hope that no one will give up on us. No matter how sinful our past or how long we've been "gone," Jesus loves us and waits for us to repent and come home. Romans 5:8 says that, "God demonstrates His own love toward us, in that while we were yet sinners, Christ died for us." Yet as we repent, we receive new life. The promise of eternity is given in Romans 6:23, "For the wages of sin is death, but the free gift of God is eternal life in Christ Jesus our Lord." He knows our real name. He loves us and wants us to share in the inheritance waiting all who believe. *Jesus is waiting . . .*

The Passage:

Read Ecclesiastes 3:6-7. Write down key points from the text and journal your thoughts about what you have read:

____

____

____

The Details:

1. What do the comparisons in verse six make you think of? Have you searched for something and given up, or thrown away something you held onto for a long time? Describe:

____

____

____

Now imagine the most sinful person. Would God give up on him or her? If the sinner repented of his sins, how would God react?

____

____

God will never give up on us. He will never leave us or forsake us. He waits for us to humble ourselves and reach out for His hand.

2. What do you think Solomon was referring to in verse seven?

Write about a time when you spoke up about something important and another time when you had to be silent:

"The fear of the LORD is the beginning of wisdom, and the knowledge of the Holy One is understanding."

Proverbs 9:10

A Closer Look:

Verse six reminds me how lost we are until the Lord saves us. God loves us so much and wants us to find his gift of salvation. He wants us to live in the freedom and hope of the good news of Jesus Christ. But we must repent. We must believe. We have to choose. You, me, and every other human this side of the Fall has had a simple, yet critical, decision: choose God or walk away. Repent and receive or face judgment. What will we choose? What will the generations choose?

We know that one day, when the Lord brings final judgment, those who are in Christ will be found in the Book of Life. Those who do not accept Jesus as the Son of God will face judgment, and will receive the same sentence that Satan himself has secured; eternal damnation. Now, that isn't a very popular thing to say in today's generation, but it is truth. It is fact. This promise from the Lord is found throughout the Scriptures, and is a definite reality.

In light of this reality, it is interesting to go through the third chapter of Ecclesiastes and read the points being made. Whether in plenty or in lack, in life or in death, happiness or sorrow, broken or mended, there is something that will last longer than our lives. It is eternity. All too often people will read this passage of Scripture and assume that there is nothing past death, and nothing that is worthwhile. Oh, there is so much waiting for those who believe! God awaits our arrival in His heavenly kingdom.

A Question for Your Life Today:

Read Matthew 28:19-20. According to those two verses, what should be our focus as we serve the Lord?

____

____

____

DAY FOUR

Serve, Work, or Toil? – Ecclesiastes 3:8-10

The Focus Verse:

I have seen the task which God has given the sons of men with which to occupy themselves. **Ecclesiastes 3:10**

The Main Thought:

Are we busy or are we obedient?

The Story within the Story:

Sister Sally Sue does everything in the church. She's too busy, but in her mind, she's doing it for God. She cooks meals for the sick, makes the tablecloths for the dinners, washes the dishes, and cleans the halls. Sally makes posters, makes copies, does newsletters, and makes drama costumes. She mans the office, drives the van, and helps with the youth group and the nursery. This sweet sister serves cookies and punch to the elderly one day and cookies and juice to the kids the next. On Sunday she teaches the kids, sings in the choir, makes announcements, and takes up requests. Every day she is just plain busy for the Lord. *Oh, the Lord will be so happy!* She sings in her spirit. *Oh, the Lord needs me so!* Her pride coos from deep within her mind. She is so busy being busy that she can't hear the whisper of God through her humming and whistling that goes on as she works. While Sally Sue is a happy, busy woman, she is also a daughter who is too busy to listen to the Father.

Service to the Lord isn't bad, and it certainly isn't wrong. Serving the Lord and others is a critical part of our community of faith and an integral part of our calling as believers. But if in our zealousness, we try to do *everything* and please everybody, we will find that nothing gets done in a way that honors God. Our family will suffer. Our church will only benefit until the time when we crash and burn. And most importantly, other people won't fill roles in the church if we take over everything ourselves! We have to be mindful to obey the Lord in doing only what He has called us to do . . . not what we pile on our plate to gain approval.

God has a place for all of us, and in His calling and plan for our lives, it will be a place of balance—a place of peace and a relationship that gives as much time to building our own relationship with the Lord as it does to pouring out in service to the world around us. The service we give is an outpouring of the fruit which comes from our time resting in the Lord. A busy body isn't necessarily a godly body!

The Passage:

Read Ecclesiastes 3:8-10. Write down key points from the text and journal your thoughts about what you have read:

The Details:

1. What does verse eight share with us?

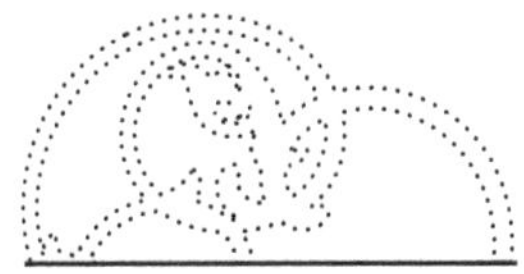

"But when the kindness of God our Savior and *His* love for mankind appeared, He saved us, not on the basis of deeds which we have done in righteousness, but according to His mercy, by the washing of regeneration and renewing by the Holy Spirit, whom He poured out upon us richly through Jesus Christ our Savior, so that being justified by His grace we would be made heirs according to the hope of eternal life."

Titus 3:4-7
[*Emphasis added.*]

This is the last association made in this passage. Why do you think it is placed last in this list? Journal your thoughts about how God can help us with these issues.

______

______

______

The type of *love* described in this verse is *ahab* love. Ahab refers to our desire for another; a strong emotional attachment that shows our approval of them. The opposite, *sane* or *hate*, infers that someone wants nothing to do with the other person. Such differences truly bring forth peace or war. No matter the era, the argument, or the generation. Love binds together; hate tears apart.

2. The writer makes an interesting shift from comparison to proclamation. What is the statement made in verses 9-10? Why do you think he stated such a thought right after the last seven verses?

______

______

______

However we work, and whatever we do, eventually we will stop working. Someday, we will all retire, and eventually we will leave this life. What impact are we making? Let's make an eternal impact. Let's leave a legacy, mentor the next generation, teach our children, and nurture others in the faith. We are to make a kingdom impact here on earth, and then for eternity.

Ecclesiastes 3:9-10 shows us the frustration someone can feel if he tried to figure out the ways of God. God's ways are not our ways and His plans are not our plans. Solomon spent the book of Ecclesiastes searching for ways to explain the wisdom of God and the ways of man. Man can't make an eternal impact unless he is connected to the eternal God. Everything else is just futile.

A Closer Look:

As we stop trying to figure out how to replace God, and quit attempting to bring peace outside of His presence, we will begin to understand the source of wisdom. Our best laid plans do not bring peace unless the Lord is the foundation of our actions.

Only God can bring true peace. God is the source of real love; without His presence, a genuine love cannot exist. No manner of earthly wisdom can replace God.

Striving to do everything in our own strength will leave us empty and without peace and love. Allowing God to be the Lord of our lives and the focus of every action and interaction will bring forth a blessed life on earth and give us a glimpse of the magnitude of God's love that awaits us in heaven.

A Question for Your Life Today:

Ecclesiastes 3:1-10 describes a wonderful series of ways to balance life. Is your life balanced, or are you struggling with too much time spent in any season listed in the passage? If so, which area?

____

____

____

DAY FIVE

God's Gift – Ecclesiastes 3:11-14

The Focus Verse:

Moreover, that every man who eats and drinks sees good in all his labor—it is the gift of God. Ecclesiastes 3:13

The Main Thought:

Get ready. Get Set. Eternity!

The Story within the Story:

While our lives come and go, and our work here on earth passes away, Solomon reminds us in today's passage that God is eternal. His ways go beyond our days on earth. His goal is our eternal standing. If we live in the light of eternity, we will live within the wisdom of God.

We've spent a week comparing the ways of the world and the inevitable seasons we will face. God is not moved by time, emotion, or earthly wisdom. As we tap into God, we tap into the things that last more than a lifetime. We will begin to set our days, our motives, and our goals on things that please the heart of God. We will begin to set our minds on things above.

Our world will present ideas and concepts to us that sound good, but lack the power and truth of God. While it may look promising, full of hope, and totally godly, if the wisdom spoken does not line up with the word of God, it is nothing more than empty promises. Pleasing God, often times, will not line up with the popular rhetoric of the day—but it will always line up with the Bible.

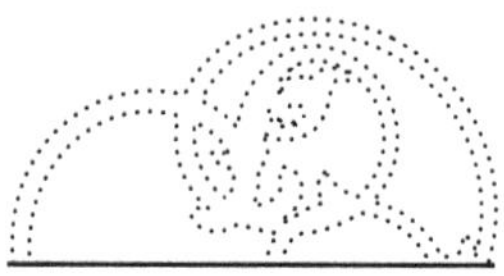

"Preach the word; be ready in season *and* out of season; reprove, rebuke, exhort, with great patience and instruction. For the time will come when they will not endure sound doctrine; but *wanting* to have their ears tickled, they will accumulate for themselves teachers in accordance to their own desires, and will turn away their ears from the truth and will turn aside to myths."

2 Timothy 4:2-4

The Passage:

Read Ecclesiastes 3:11-14. Write down key points from the text and journal your thoughts about what you have read:

____

____

____

The Details:

1. According to verse 11, along with appropriate seasons, what else has God done?

____

____

____

____

Even with this provision, do we understand all He has done?

____

____

____

2. What encouragement we have in verses 12-13! Even though life comes and goes, how are we supposed to view our work?

____

____

____

3. What do we learn about God in verse 14?

____

____

____

The end of verse 14 tells us the purpose of God's ways—why has He done everything?

____

____

____

God's ultimate goal in our lives is to bring forth relationship between Himself and His people, and for believers to fear Him. Fear, or *yare*, speaks of a reverence that comes from our desire and devotion for our God.

A Closer Look:

As Solomon ended this book of Ecclesiastes, he made this final observation:

"The conclusion, when all has been heard, is: fear God and keep His commandments, because this applies to every person. For God will bring every act to judgment, everything which is hidden, whether good or evil" (Ecclesiastes 12:13-14).

After all the comparisons and the chapters following our focus passage that talk about the miseries of life and the futility of our actions, Solomon tells us the bottom line is, fear God, keep His commands; judgment will come.

A Question for Your Life Today:

In light of this week's lesson, how would you encourage someone who is going through a difficult season in life?

____

____

____

____

____

WORKS CITED:

Baker, Warren and Eugene Carpenter, eds. *The Complete Word Study Dictionary: Old Testament.* Chattanooga: AMG Publishers, 2003:

Zeman, #2165, p. 294-295

Ahab, #157, p. 20

Sane, #8130, p. 1175-1176

Yare, #3372, p. 470

WEEK SIX

Most High God

The Greatness of God

Isaiah 40:10-31

In a moment of desperation, a season of wondering why he was leading a stubborn people, Moses shows us another side of following God: learning to seek, find, and praise God for who He is. In Exodus 33 we find the account of Moses in the midst of his journey with the Lord calling out to His God with boldness and asking to see the glory of the Lord Most High. Moses has had fellowship with God, but He wants more. He needs to *know* God, to *see* God, and to *be known* as a man who follows the Father. In and of itself, this request is bold, but in context, Moses' request comes at an interesting moment; after the first set of Ten Commandment tablets are given, after the calf idol was crafted by Aaron and the people, and after Moses smashes the tablets of the law in a moment of rage.

I can hear Moses' passion for the Lord as he intercedes for his own life and the stubborn people who follow him. *Please Lord, spare them, Lord. Let me know your ways, God. Don't forget your people. Set us apart. I want to see your glory.* Exodus 33:16 reveals the heartbeat of an obedient heart, as Moses cries out:

> How then can it be known that I have found favor in Your sight, I and Your people? Is it not by Your going with us, so that we, I and Your people, may be distinguished from all the *other* people who are upon the face of the earth? [Emphasis added.]

Did you catch that? Moses understood that in order to be a people of God, the Hebrews had to be distinguished from everyone else. *They had to be different.* Followers of God don't look like the world. Why? Because God is bigger than anything we know in all of humanity. Our God is not some block of wood we carve or a statue made out of metal. Our Lord and Savior surpasses any false god created in the imagination of man. The Lord is more powerful than any power, kingdom, leader, military, civil movement, earthly wisdom, or race of people. God is mighty, and there is none like Him.

How did God proclaim His glory to Moses? Listen to the Word of the Lord:

> The LORD, the LORD God, compassionate and gracious, slow to anger, and abounding in lovingkindness and truth; who keeps lovingkindness for thousands, who forgives iniquity, transgression and sin; yet He will by no means leave *the guilty* unpunished, visiting the iniquity of fathers on the children and on the grandchildren to the third and fourth generations (Exodus 34:6-7). [*Emphasis added.*]

This is how God proclaims His glory. These are God's words and God's announcement. The quote above is the timeless definition of the Lord. It was first spoken to Moses, but applies to Isaiah's generation and to us today.

As we will see with this week's lesson, there is no one like our God. The Lord used Isaiah to bring comfort to His people through encouragement to be strong and to not lose hope. By focusing on the majesty of the Lord, the people would understand the source of their strength. We serve a great and mighty God who longs for us to know His greatness.

DAY ONE

Our Shepherd – Isaiah 40:10-17

The Focus Verse:

***Like a shepherd He will tend His flock, in His arm He will gather the lambs, and carry them in His bosom; He will gently lead the nursing ewes.* Isaiah 40:11**

The Main Thought:

The Almighty God cares for us.

The Story within the Story:

Moses led the Israelites out of captivity and into the wilderness. The Lord showed Him the way, provided for their needs, and gave them the Law. Manna, quail, water from a rock, and safe passage through the sea—the Lord's provision was varied and timely. Yet the people rebelled. Moses continued to shepherd the flock that the Lord gave to him, regardless of what they did to disobey and disrespect the Lord. Moses, the Lord's shepherd, followed the cloud and the fire, following his God's lead.

Jesus, our Great Shepherd, guides our path. He has given us His Holy Spirit to lead us into the truth. We have a Shepherd who loves us and calls us by name. One day, He will come again, drawing His believers to Himself, and providing an eternity filled with safety and praise. A promise we should all look forward to with excited anticipation and thankful hearts. We have a Shepherd who loves us, and provides for our needs before we even know to ask.

The Passage:

Read Isaiah 40:10-17. Write down key points from the text and journal your thoughts about what you have read:

____

____

____

The Details:

1. What does Isaiah 40:10 say about how the Lord will come?

____

____

____

This verse refers to the Second Coming of Jesus Christ. We read that He will come with power, and that He will rule and bring reward.

2. In verse 11, what is God described like? Who does He care for?

____

____

____

God will care for His people as the shepherd cares for his sheep. Remember our discussion of John 10? Jesus is our Great Shepherd, the gate to all who believe in the gospel. He knows our voice, He knows our heart. Jesus directs our steps, and keeps us safe.

3. Isaiah 40:12 gives a great description of the omnipotence (all powerful nature) of God. What does it describe?

____

____

____

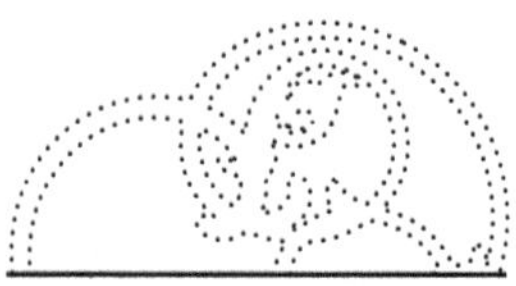

"The grass withers, the flower fades, but the word of our God stands forever."

Isaiah 40:8

Our Creator God measured the heavens, made the boundaries for the waterlines, and established the magnificent mountains. Going back to our first chapter together, we know that He is the God of all Creation.

4. Isaiah 40:13-14 speaks of the Holy Spirit and wisdom. Note the qualities of the Lord that are pointed out in these two verses:

____

____

____

____

5. Read verses 15-17. What nation is greater than God? What is the position of the nations of the earth in comparison to the Lord?

____

____

____

A Closer Look:

Who gave God His wisdom? Who does the Lord answer to? God is omnipotent (all-powerful), omniscient (all-knowing), and omnipresent (always there). There is none before Him, and there will be no others beside Him. The Lord reigns supreme over all the earth. No nation is greater than He; no offering surpasses His gift of Jesus Christ.

This theme of God's power and position as the one true God is woven throughout Scripture. It is truth, and everything in the Bible hinges on this fact. The life of a believer also depends on faith in this truth. We serve a mighty God!

A Question for Your Life Today:

Here we are at the end of our journey together. We began with the Creation account, and we are finishing with Isaiah's great description of our Almighty God. Looking at our passage in Isaiah 40:10-31, list some of the ways Isaiah describes the greatness of God:

____

____

____

____

____

____

DAY TWO

Incomparable Savior – Isaiah 40:15-20

The Focus Verse:

To whom then will you liken God? Or what likeness will you compare with Him? **Isaiah 40:18**

The Main Thought:

Who can compare with the Lord?

The Story within the Story:

"I have a red car."

"Well, I have a bigger red car with racing stripes."

"Oh, really? Mine has doors that open and a steering wheel that moves!"

"So! Mine races forward. Watch this . . ."

Sound familiar? The competitive argument over childhood toys isn't much different from some of our adult conversations. Just read the local paper. Our newspaper has a weekly section on faith. What once had many announcements and stories on the Christian faith now contains a myriad of articles trying to share the experiences of other paths of religion. It has slowly become a breeding ground for comparison shopping and political correctness.

Each week, the newspaper section is filled with columns inviting us to join in with the various celebrations held in our community—no matter what faith you choose. More than truly sticking to a single belief, the trend of these articles asserts that we all follow the same thing—one Supreme Being. If all the false gods are lumped together, is it really a supreme being? And, if we try to combine all the false religions with

Christianity, lowering God to the level of these humanistic gods, does our "God" still hold any form of true divinity? This passage in Isaiah boldly tells us what we should already know. God is above all other gods, and cannot be compared to a deity made in the hands and minds of man.

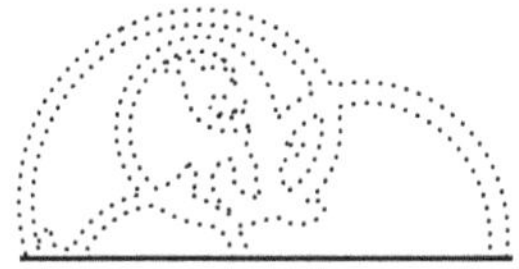

"Hear, O Israel! The LORD is our God, the LORD is one! You shall love the LORD your God with all your heart and with all your soul and with all your might."

Deuteronomy 6:4-5

The Passage:

Read Isaiah 40:15-20. Write down key points from the text and journal your thoughts about what you have read:

The Details:

1. Write out Isaiah 40:18:

Our Jehovah God is truly incomparable. There is none like Him. How does this verse impact your life today? What issues, problems, sins, or fears are standing between you and this statement? What has taken a more important position in your life than God?

Take a moment for prayer and reflection. Ask the Lord to help you conquer sinful patterns, rise above earthly problems, and live in the peace that comes from making the Lord the highest *priority* and *authority* in your life.

2. Verses 19 and 20 show the process of creation for false idols. How are they made?

____

____

____

Idols are made of wood, metal, clay, or other materials fashioned by man into the image they want to worship. Somehow the idol worshiper is blinded from the fact that the idol made by his own hands has no power at all. Only God can save and only the Lord hears us when we call.

At the end of verse 20, when it says "an idol that will not totter," they are referring to the necessity for a firmly-based piece to keep the idol from falling over. The false god cannot stand by itself, nor can it help the follower stand in time of trouble. It has no power!

A Closer Look:

Our God does not need our help to stand. He does not need us to carve His image. We worship Jesus Christ in spirit and in truth. The God of the Bible is the Creator, not something made or imagined by creation. If we look at the many religions in our world today, we will see many different types of idols, statues, and worshiped items. We will see people revering animals higher than the Lord; self awareness and personal wisdom above the Holy Spirit; and a connectivity of false faiths that is deemed to be more critical than standing for the truths of Scripture. Careful! We do not serve a God made by man—and a unity that rules out the God of the Bible is nothing more than a modern day attempt to rebuild the Tower of Babel.

A Question for Your Life Today:

How do these descriptions confirm the God of Creation from Chapter One?

____

____

____

____

DAY THREE

Hear Ye, Hear Ye! – Isaiah 40:21-24

The Focus Verse:

Do you not know? Have you not heard? Has it not been declared to you from the beginning? Have you not understood from the foundations of the earth? **Isaiah 40:21**

The Main Thought:

Do you not know?

The Story within the Story:

The gossip mill is an amazing thing. One person learns a juicy story, and shares it with two friends. They won't tell . . . or will they? Next thing you know, the whole group of friends is in on the secret. A week later, the whole church knows the scoop. Prayers go out, concerns are shared, and mouths hidden behind the screen of a hand project information into closely positioned listening ears. *Secrets.* Can't live with them, the world can't seem to turn without them.

Is our God a secret? Can we only find out about the secrets of the Lord through initiation into a secret society or club? Do we find out about the Lord Almighty through a secret shared behind closed doors? Oh, for heaven's sake, no! The world is the stage for the message of God. No one is kept from His truth, no one is refused access to salvation *if* they hear, believe, repent, and live in the truth.

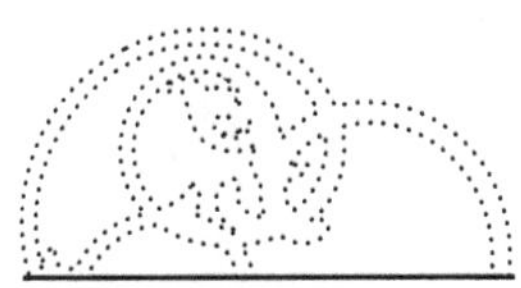

God's story is timeless. The same old story of the Bible is still *the* story of God!

God's story isn't even a new story. We don't have to run after the "newest" path to Christianity because God's path was established with creation and is timeless and without walls. He longs for the world to know Him and live in light of His truth.

Do you now know? Have you not heard? God loves you, and sent His Son to bring salvation.

The Passage:

Read Isaiah 40:21-24. Write down key points from the text and journal your thoughts about what you have read:

The Details:

1. Read Isaiah 40:21. What previous week's lesson and topic come to mind?

In this verse, all believers are reminded that God is the God of Creation. We have come back around to the first week's lesson on creation. God makes no mystery of the fact that He is the Creator of all we see and all we live amongst. He laid the foundation.

2. Reading verse 22, how is the Lord portrayed? Is He small and insignificant, or magnificent and mighty? Describe the verse, and your reaction to this portrayal of God.

Our God "sits above the vault of the earth" and stretches the heavens. We cannot comprehend the full magnitude of the Lord.

3. What do verses 23-24 reveal? What happens to those who do not follow the Lord?

Romans 1:20 tells us that, "Since the creation of the world His invisible attributes, His eternal power and divine nature, have been clearly seen, being understood through what has been made, so that they were without excuse." God has made Himself known. His gospel goes forth throughout the nations. We who hear of the truth of Jesus and walk away in search of other gods will one day stand in the judgment of the Almighty. We will be without excuse.

A Closer Look:

What better encouragement do we have than to know that our God reigns? When we are feeling defeated, weary, or just plain tired, isn't it wonderful to know that the Lord is mighty and He not only created the universe and the earth, but He cares for His creation? I find great comfort in that truth.

Those who do not worship the Creator, but settle for giving devotion to that which is created, will not have such comfort. There is no power in an idol made of wood or stone. May we be a Great Commission generation who shares the message of hope with the lost tribes of the world, and may they replace their idols with a genuine relationship with their Creator.

A Question for Your Life Today:

As you go about your daily activities, how can this passage encourage you?

DAY FOUR

Who Is His Equal? - Isaiah 40:25-27

The Focus Verse:

"To whom then will you liken Me that I would be his equal?' says the Holy One.
Isaiah 40:25

The Main Thought:

God's power spans the heavenlies.

The Story within the Story:

Growing up, I remember going to my grandmother's house and looking at the NASA stuff on the walls and shelves. Even in our own home we had knick-knacks and interesting reminders of my grandpa's adventures. Although I never met my grandfather, I have lived my life enamored with his life experiences. He was a country doctor, a military surgeon, served with NASA, and an all-around amazing guy. According to the articles, plaques, mementoes, and memories, my grandpa was right there in the midst of the space race as it geared up and shot the first rockets through the atmosphere. Grandpa was there, somewhere. How cool is that?

Somehow, this family history has revved up my interest in the technology and romantic notion of space travel. Our family frequents the museums and exhibits. Our son attends camps and activities geared for space education. My husband even works alongside aeronautical engineers, astronauts, and space station control room engineers. Somehow, God has continued to bring our family into the heritage of our country's interest in the universe God created.

Even with this fascination and involvement, do we stop at the stars? Do we think there is nothing beyond the galaxy we research? The Lord clearly shares with us that even the furthest reaches of our solar system are but a speck in His domain. He knows every hair on our head and He named every star in the sky. God looks down through space and time to care for His people. We are simply fascinated with another layer of the creation of the Lord.

The Passage:

Read Isaiah 40:25-27. Write down key points from the text and journal your thoughts about what you have read:

The Details:

1. Isaiah 40:25 repeats the theme of the sovereignty of God. How is this truth conveyed in this verse?

Again the question beckons: "Who is like the Lord?" My friend, no one is like the Lord. Nothing compares. There is no other like the Holy One. The use of the term "Holy One" in this verse tracks back to the Hebrew term *qados*, which *The Complete Word Study Dictionary: Old Testament* explains as "often used to refer to God as being inherently holy, sacred, and set apart" (p. 976). No other god is sacred and holy like the God of the Bible. He is the Holy One, the Lord of all creation.

2. What portion of the creation story is affirmed in verse 26?

"Lift up your eyes on high and see who has created these *stars*, the One who leads forth their host by number, He calls them out by name; because of the greatness of His might and the strength of *His* power, not one of *them* is missing."

Isaiah 40:26 [*Emphasis added.*]

3. Verse 27 has a clear admonishment for the Israelites. What is the correction?

Nothing is hidden from the sight of God. None of our indiscretions or sins is hidden from His view. This is a clear warning to avoid hiding things from the Almighty God.

A Closer Look:

God's universe is more than we can possibly grasp. He named the stars, set the universe in place and in motion, and He knows every inch of it in detail. Nothing is hidden, especially not our own sins and false worship. God sees everything!

A Question for Your Life Today:

How can you encourage others with the truths you've learned in this study?

DAY FIVE

Have You Not Heard? – Isaiah 40:28-31

The Focus Verse:

Yet those who wait for the LORD will gain new strength; they will mount up with wings like eagles, they will run and not get tired, they will walk and not become weary. **Isaiah 40:31**

The Main Thought:

God is our strength.

The Story within the Story:

"I just can't go on. Not one more step. I'm done."

Ever muttered those words? Ever thought you were at your wit's end and unable to take another step? Me, too. Years ago in a galaxy of fitness far, far away, I enjoyed going on Volksmarches with my husband. Popular in Germany and among military communities around the world, these 10K (6 miles or so) walks through the woods are great if you like to walk—a lot.

The first event I participated in was certainly far from joyful for me. Oh, the first mile was beautiful, the second was scenic, but by mile three or four, I was ready to jump on the next bus heading for the finish line. Unfortunately, there's no bus. It's just you, your comfy shoes (which aren't so comfy by the end of the trek) and your walking stick. There's nothing but the beaten path behind you and the beckoning path in front. So, unless you want to sit a spell, the only option is forward motion.

My husband encouraged me and giggled as I complained through miles four, five, and six. Suddenly, with the finish line in view, my adrenaline kicked in and I sped up the pace. *We made it! I did it! It wasn't so bad after all.* Success. The finish line. Triumph.

Oh, how our walk with the Lord can be exciting. Oh, how life can be draining. Oh, how the finish line, our entrance to heaven, is the triumph that will carry us through eternity.

The Passage:

Read Isaiah 40:28-31. Write down key points from the text and journal your thoughts about what you have read:

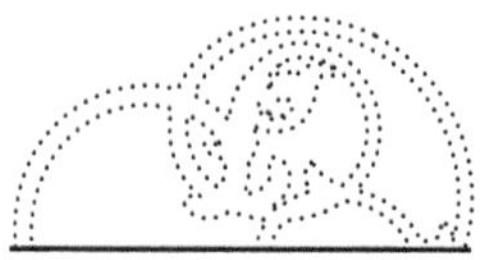

"Do you not know? Have you not heard? The Everlasting God, the Lord, the Creator of the ends of the earth does not become weary or tired. His understanding is inscrutable."

Isaiah 40:28

The Details:

1. Verse 28 is a wonderful proclamation of the Lord's strength and majesty. What does the verse proclaim?

God does not tire or grow weary. He is not limited in strength or understanding!

2. What does Isaiah 40:29 reveal about how the Lord provides strength to His followers?

God gives strength and power to those in need. Describe a time when you have felt the Lord give you strength when it was needed, and power when you have needed it:

____

____

____

3. The most recognized verse in our lesson this week is verse 31. Where have you heard this verse used? What does it mean to you?

____

____

____

Look at the different principles in Isaiah 40:31. We need to:

- ____________________ for the Lord.
- We will ______________________________ .
- We will mount up with wings like ____________________ .
- We will ____________________ and not get tired.
- We will ____________________ and not become weary.

A Closer Look:

God provides strength and power in our time of need. The first portion of Isaiah 40:31 talks about waiting for the Lord. The Hebrew translation for this phrase is *qawah* or "putting our hope and confidence in something." As we trust in the Lord, and wait for Him to deliver us, we will be strengthened by His power, and blessed by His provision.

Mounting up on wings as eagles gives us the picture of the Lord raising us above our weariness and causing us to rise above any hardship we are facing. When the Lord draws us to Himself at the end of the age, and we spend eternity in His presence, we will no longer experience any fatigue or weariness. We will be strengthened by

His spirit, and will have a glorified body that never wears out. Rejoice in the hope of eternity!

I have loved traveling this journey with you for the past six weeks. I encourage you to keep seeking the Lord with all your heart and to keep learning who He is through His Word. God's Word is alive and active; it will transform your life, and the way you think about God. Keep *growing!*

Much love in Christ,

Jennifer

A Question for Your Life Today:

Take some time and reflect on the things you've learned in this study guide. How have the verses changed the way you think about God?

____

____

____

How have they changed the way you view yourself in relationship to God and others?

____

____

____

Before you end your time of study today, pray for God to reveal even more details to you about the verses you know by heart. Thank you for joining us on this journey!

WORKS CITED:

Baker, Warren and Eugene Carpenter, eds. *The Complete Word Study Dictionary: Old Testament.* Chattanooga: AMG Publishers, 2003:

Qados, #6918, p. 976-977

Qawah, #6960, p. 986

Note to Leaders

Visit **www.randallhouse.com** and receive a free Leader's Guide for *Verses We Know by Heart*. Discover tools to aid you in leading your church or small study group through a six-week journey that will cultivate a deeper walk with God. In this on-line resource you will find teacher thoughts, quick questions, and suggested extras for each week. You will also find a personal letter from Jennifer Devlin.